Raise Your Game

How to succeed at work

Peter Shaw

CAPSTONE

(ISBN) 978-1-906-46553-7

A catalogue record for this book is available from the British Library.

Set in 11 on 13 pt Photina MT by SNP Best-set Typesetter Ltd., Hong Kong
Printed in Great Britain by TJ International Ltd, Padstow, Cornwall

Dedicated to our daughter Ruth, who through her encouragement and practical wisdom enables others to build effectively on their strengths, to grow in confidence and to take on bigger challenges than they had ever thought possible.

Contents

Acknowledgements

One of the greatest joys of coaching work is seeing people raise their game and step up to take on bigger and more demanding roles successfully. All the people I work with have influenced my thinking. I am grateful to them for giving me the privilege of spending time working with them and giving me the joy of seeing them grow and develop.

I have talked to many people about ideas in the book. Those who have had a particular influence include Paul West, Brian Leveson, Julie Taylor, Louise Tulett, John Suffolk, Mel Zuydam, Kevin White, Una O'Brien, Tom McLaughlan, Andrew Hudson, Tony Dean, Finlay Scott, Archie Hughes, Judith Macgregor, Melanie Dawes, Anna Walker, June Milligan, Gordon MacDonald, Hazel Mackenzie, Jane Frost, Martin Oakley, Martin Sinclair, Adele Townsend, Jeremy Oates, Sarah Walker, Oliver Rowe, Chetan Patel, Fiona Spencer, Sunil Patel, John Pritchard, Dominic Jermey, Penny Ciniewicz, Jonathan Slater, Paula Higson, Lesley Strathie, Hugh Taylor and Igor Judge. I take full responsibility for the views in the book but the perspectives of those above have been especially influential.

I am grateful to a number of people who read the manuscript and gave me clear comments. The observations of Mairi Eastwood, Heather Dawson, Zoe Stear and Hilary Douglas have been invaluable in ensuring the text is clear and structured.

I am grateful to Suma Chakrabarti for contributing the foreword to this book. I have always found Suma a constructive and thoughtful leader who has stepped up through a sequence of demanding jobs to become one of the most influential Permanent Secretaries in government. I have always been grateful for Suma's encouragement both when in government and now in coaching and writing.

I am grateful to John Wiley for their practical support. Sarah Sutton commissioned the book, Emma Swaisland has taken it forward to publication and Jenny Ng has looked after the detailed arrangements for publication.

My Executive Assistant, Claire Pratt, has managed the diary with considerable foresight to ensure that I have been able to slot in conversations with a wide range of people in preparing the book. Jackie Tookey and Tracy Easthope have typed the manuscript, slotting it into their other work. They have always been cheerful and helpful.

I am grateful to my colleagues at Praesta Partners who always bring practical advice and a level-headed approach. We learn a great deal from each other because of our diverse backgrounds and different approaches.

My family are an important source of encouragement in the writing. It has been such a joy for Frances and me to see our children step up to take on a wide range of different responsibilities in their chosen spheres. This book is dedicated to our daughter, Ruth, who is always perceptive and wise. Her generosity and kindness have been an encouragement to many friends and colleagues as they have been raising their game to cope with new and demanding situations.

Finally, raising your game is not just about your own efforts. It flows from the encouragement, support and stretch of others. Those who have particularly helped me raise my game in my second career of coaching and writing have been Mairi Eastwood, Robin Linnecar, Liz Walmsley, Paul Gray, Hilary Douglas and Claire Pratt. To them, and all the people I work with, I say a big thank you.

Foreword

When I observe an individual growing successfully into a larger role I am delighted. Seeing
an individual fully realise their potential is one
of the biggest satisfactions of leadership. Why do
some people raise their game successfully while
others appear to struggle?

Peter Shaw has written a definitive guide to raising
your game and achieving your full potential. He suggests
that progress results from a blend of belief that comes
from inner confidence and clarity of values, alongside
practical action that is realistic, determined and planned.
He talks persuasively of the balance between being and
doing. Being is about thinking yourself fully into the role
and doing is the practical behaviour and action that
underpins success.

The book draws on a wealth of examples from individuals in different sectors. Peter's approach is as relevant to
a junior manager as a chief executive. The sequence of
short, focused chapters conclude with suggested practical
actions that are always rooted in reality and ambitious.
One of the distinctive contributions of the book is the list
of questions that readers are invited to ask themselves

under each theme: a few minutes' reflection on the questions in each chapter will always be worthwhile.

Peter draws on a wealth of experience as a director general in government and as an executive coach and facilitator. He brings both clarity and humanity into his coaching and his writing. Peter and I first met 15 years ago and our paths have crossed many times since. He has always been a source of encouragement to me. I know from those he coaches that his supportive and yet stretching approach is greatly appreciated. Many speak warmly of his coaching and as a result have raised their game in ways beyond their expectations.

Raise Your Game is the latest in a sequence of books by Peter that encapsulates the approach he uses in coaching in such a way that a wider audience can benefit. I commend this book wholeheartedly and I am sure that many will raise their game effectively as a result of putting ideas from the book into practice.

**Suma Chakrabarti, Permanent Secretary,
Ministry of Justice**

Introduction

We live in an ever more demanding world. The speed of change is relentless. Global economics and new technology mean that decisions are taken ever more quickly. Success and failure are close companions. Shocks and surprises come in many different shapes and sizes. Long-term values and expectations are continually being questioned.

Today, the environment for everyone in every sector is tougher and more challenging than it has been for many years. We sort out one challenge and then there is another one to address. How can we be at our best in challenging times? When it is really tough over an extended period, what will keep us going so that we can make good decisions, give our best and be creative at work, and make a contribution to other spheres of life that are important to us?

How can you best raise your game and achieve your full potential when the pace of change is fast and the demands on you are considerable? Personal growth and survival depend on how you handle relentless challenge. You can feel at the mercy of external pressures. It can seem like three steps forward and two steps back. How do you raise your game when you feel frustrated, buffeted, ignored and weary?

Those who are able to raise their game can become influential beyond their expectations. Those who can rise above turbulence and provide focused, measured and calm leadership can create a new sense of direction and renewed energy.

The pace of change creates opportunities as well as frustrations.

Success comes from taking control of what you can control while accepting what you cannot control. It is recognising when you do have a choice, even if it is only the choice of what you think about an issue. Success flows from keeping a positive frame of mind and not wallowing in misfortune.

The issue for you

So how can you ensure that you step up and raise your game effectively? How can you build on your strengths and ensure that you can get a grip on your responsibilities quickly and smoothly? Sometimes you feel daunted and there is an element of self-doubt. What are the next steps you need to take? How do you up the pace and keep a life?

Maybe you are about to start a new job, which you are looking forward to. Maybe your job is going faster and faster and you have to run to keep up. What will make the crucial difference to your skills, your behaviour and your attitudes to help ensure that you will step up successfully and enjoy those further responsibilities?

This book will enable you to become more confident so that you learn and thrive as well as enjoy what you do.

It provides a practical tool kit for raising your game and stepping up successfully. Do you resonate with the experiences of Miranda, Mary or John?

The Newly Promoted

Miranda was a confident and successful manager. She had grown in self-assurance during three years in her role and had been seeking promotion. Following a successful promotion board, she felt both excitement and apprehension. She was thrilled to have been promoted and knew that she would be able to do the job well. But there was a touch of apprehension, which she saw as positive as it would keep her alert to the expectations of those around her. Miranda knew she would need to step up and was keen to ensure that she found the best way of doing so successfully.

The Confidence Factor

Mary knows she has a great deal to offer. She has a good degree, excellent professional qualifications, a mentor who believes in her and a track record of success, but there is a continual sense of frustration. In meetings her confidence seems to evaporate. She experiences a touch of self-doubt and she becomes hesitant. Her strength of conviction is dissipated and the resolve she had when she entered the meeting seems to disappear out of the window. How can she raise her game so that she makes the impact she knows she is capable of?

The Overlooked Potential

John feels that his life is a continual struggle. He works hard but he seems to get nowhere. One day he is praised and another day he is ignored. John doesn't seem to be able to make the impact he wants. He yearns to know how to step up successfully so that he can turn his ideas into successful business outcomes. He wants to raise his game, but he doesn't always know how best to do so. He is aware that if he doesn't do something soon to make a difference, he may well be overlooked for promotion or, worse still, forced out.

Being and Doing

I suggest that the way forward is a powerful blend of two key concepts:

- Self-belief that comes from a combination of inner confidence and clarity of values; alongside
- Practical action that is realistic, determined and planned.

At the heart of this book is the balance between being and doing. *Being* is about becoming comfortable in your skin whatever role you are in. *Doing* is about the practical behaviours and steps that underpin success.

Being is thinking yourself into the role so that you fill the space of the leader or manager you want to be in a confident and effective way. Doing is about techniques that enable you to do this effectively.

Being is about:

- Embedding your values
- Knowing your strengths
- Believing you can step up
- Being confident in yourself and your role
- Keeping an open mind
- Being clear what matters to you
- Knowing what difference you want to make
- Knowing what will give you joy

Doing includes:

- Developing your strengths
- Understanding your least strong areas and knowing how best to live with them
- Creating an equilibrium in the way you work that is successful for you
- Building your network of supporters and stakeholders
- Growing your resilience
- Knowing how to use your time well
- Being practical in using your energy in a focused way

Both the being and doing dimensions are crucial to success. The interplay between them is also vital.

In addition, this book considers six phases that occur as you raise your game:

- *Take stock*, which looks at developing your strengths, understanding your least strong areas embedding your values, and creating your equilibrium.
- *First steps*, which involves addressing your fears, believing you can do difficult things, knowing who your supporters and stakeholders are and the learning that comes from taking some risks.

xviii   Raise Your Game: How to succeed at work

- *Up the pace*, which embraces stretching your muscles, growing your supporters and converting your critics, understanding how you respond to problems and warming down thoroughly.
- *Grow the momentum*, which includes keeping your focus, growing your resilience, building your team and renewing your freshness.
- *Where next*, which embraces keeping an open mind, recognising when the tide turns, knowing what matters to you and renewing your vision.
- *To what end*, which covers the difference you want to make, how you want to be remembered, the relevance of family and friends and where joy fits in.

The combined effect of taking forward the being and doing dimensions is to create the prospect of a sequence of step changes that mean you will raise your game and achieve your full potential. What is so important is embedding your learning and thinking it through with colleagues, a mentor or a coach.

Next Steps

The book draws from the practical experiences of individuals in a variety of different spheres, embracing the private, public and voluntary sectors. The common advice from all of them is:

- Be active in identifying and building on your strengths.
- Know what your values are and test your actions against those values.
- Be willing to take risks and be bold and adventurous in your approach while being rooted in practical realism.

- Set your sights high while recognising that the journey will be one step at a time.
- Recognise the choices you have.
- Build a network of supporters who will give you encouragement and constructive challenges.
- Be self-aware enough to know when you are being driven in a way that is more likely to take you to 'death rather than glory'.

Paul West, the Chief Constable of West Mercia Police, summarises what he observes in people who step up successfully as:

> *They can understand strategy and are able to simplify it and make it relevant for their staff. They are capable of taking a corporate view and avoid 'silo' working. They are willing to delegate but do not abdicate responsibility. They are skilled in networking and managing relationships. They are good at coaching and developing others and are open-minded to things being done differently. In terms of their own performance, they are receptive to constructive criticism, advice and feedback.'*

You can read this book from start to finish or by looking at specific sections that relate to your needs and circumstances. I strongly encourage you to use the book as a basis for discussion with a friend, a colleague, a mentor, a coach or within your team. Even if the best way of learning for you is to reflect on something inside yourself, it is as you speak your thoughts

As you articulate your thoughts and actions they become embedded.

and actions to someone else that you embed them and commit yourself to take them forward. Do enjoy this book as you raise your game and step up to take on new and different challenges successfully.

Peter Shaw
Godalming, January 2009

Section A
Take Stock

This section is about taking stock. You need to start by being honest with yourself:

- *Develop your strengths*
- *Understand your least strong areas*
- *Embed your values*
- *Create an equilibrium*

As you read through each chapter, do reflect on where you are in relation to each of these themes and what might be the next steps for you. You may need to identify the strengths you want to build on further; understand your least strong areas more fully, which allows you to decide how you want to address them; crystallise your values, which can give you greater confidence in difficult situations; or be clearer about what equilibrium works best for you to enable you to use your time and energy to best effect.

Chapter 1
Develop Your Strengths

Knowing your strengths provides a sound basis for building for the future. They are the best basis on which you can build. You need to recognise your strengths, grow your strengths, observe your strengths and look after your strengths. Strengths need nurturing and cannot just be taken for granted. Strengths are not just what we perceive about ourselves but are what others perceive about the particular qualities we bring.

Why are strengths important?

There is a danger that you are not accurately aware of your strengths and talents. Often, as people grow, they become experts in describing their own weaknesses and spend time trying to address these faults rather than building on their strengths. As a result, some of their strengths can lay hidden and ignored, with the consequence that they are undeveloped and dissipate over time.

When you are fully aware of your strengths and confident in them, you are able to do things that you might have been much more hesitant about in the past. As you use your strengths you become ever more confident in their value and application.

Recognise your strengths

A good starting point is to articulate what you think your strengths are. You can supplement this by honestly summarising what you think other key people, such as your family, colleagues and boss, would regard as your strengths.

I recently asked one leader what he thought his strengths were. He said:

- Good awareness of the environment around him
- Good at building on different strengths in others
- Good at problem solving
- An empathy for the emotional reactions of other people
- Good technical and professional skills
- A good ambassador for the organisation

He said that his family would regard his strengths as:

- Putting them first
- Having a strong family commitment
- Showing financial prudence

He thought that the people who worked for him would describe his strengths as:

- Accessibility
- Decisiveness

- Clarity of what he wanted from them
- Setting high standards
- Giving people confidence
- Being somebody whom others could talk to in confidence

He thought that his boss would describe his strengths as:

- The ability to carry a heavy load
- Effective problem solving ability
- Providing a safe pair of hands
- Being a good representative and a dependable professional

Looking at your strengths through different perspectives allows you to begin to see yourself *as others see you*. At one level you can do this by imagining yourself standing in other people's shoes and commenting on your strengths. Another approach is to ask people directly what they perceive as your strengths, or to request a colleague or coach to ask them on your behalf. You might be able to use the kind of 360° written feedback tool that many organisations have available for their staff.

It can help to write a list covering:

- What do you think are your five key strengths?
- What do you think your colleagues would see as your five key strengths?
- What would your close family members or friends see as your strengths?

Another approach is to look at generic lists of strengths and assess which might apply particularly to you. In their excellent book *Now, Discover your Strengths* (Pocket Books, 2004), Marcus Buckingham and Donald Clifton talk about each individual needing to become an expert at finding, describing, applying, practising and refining their strengths. They talk of distinguishing natural talents from things you can learn and seeing strengths as a combination of talents, knowledge and skills. To them, talents are your naturally recurring patterns of thought, feeling or behaviour, with knowledge consisting of the facts and lessons learned, and skills as the steps of an activity. These authors' approach is to encourage the reader to identify their five strongest themes of talent, some of which may not be strengths as yet. They identify the 34 themes of the Strengthsfinder profile, which are set out in Box 1.

Working on an illustrative list of strengths such as the one referred to in Box 1 can be helpful in reminding you of aspects you might not have perceived as strengths.

Grow your strengths

Your strengths never stand still. You are either growing them or, if you allow them to stagnate, they will be declining in effectiveness. As you look back you can often see how your strengths have been changing. You can identify the strengths that have been consistently a valuable part of your armoury and those that have adapted and grown as a consequence of circumstances and experience.

John Suffolk held senior positions in the private sector before moving into central government roles and has now done two very significant jobs within central gov-

---

Box 1 The Thirty Four Themes of the Strengthsfinder® Profile

Achiever	Futuristic
Activator	Harmony
Adaptability	Ideation
Analytical	Includer
Arranger	Individualisation
Belief	Input
Command	Intellection
Communication	Learner
Competition	Maximizer
Connectedness	Positivity
Consistency	Relator
Context	Responsibility
Deliberative	Restorative
Developer	Self-assurance
Discipline	Significance
Empathy	Strategic
Focus	Woo

StrengthsFinder® Profile – Marcus Buckingham and Donald Clifton

ernment. When pressed about what had enabled him to step up into these senior roles, he said:

I have built up the right tools in the kit bag. I believe I can take a complex issue, simplify it, crystallise the key issues and see the big picture. I view events as an opportunity and not a threat and never give up.

John has brought his great strengths of clear thinking and clarity of purpose into his two leadership roles within government. What I have observed in John is both his use of strong, natural talent and the way he adapts that talent to the particular leadership challenges he has faced. The fact that he has brought clarity of thinking to complex issues and simplified them well has been greatly appreciated by his colleagues. The positive reinforcement of this capability to bring clarity has enabled him to use this strength and develop it further to powerful effect. John is an excellent example of someone who has natural talent and has been willing to hone that talent to meet the needs of a new context when he moved from the private to the public sector.

However effective your strengths, they need nurturing and growing. For all his natural talent, Tiger Woods still practises regularly and draws on the expertise of coaches.

Growing your strengths is about making what is good even better.

Mel Zuydam, has held senior finance director positions in both the private and public sectors. He used to see his particular strengths as on the technical and financial side rather than on the people side. In his role as a finance director within government, he developed different approaches using his strengths with people as well as his strengths on technical issues. He said that he 'crossed the Rubicon' when he realised he should use both his technical and human sets of strengths. He comments:

> *To do a job effectively as a finance director is to be consensual and bring people with you. Keeping listening is so important. To raise your game you need high-level self-awareness and you need to learn from the way others perceive you. You need to have genuine respect for what others say about you. I realised that others*

view me in a different way to the way I view myself.
Then my tool kit quadrupled in size.

Mel talks of reflecting on the right approach to use when he wants to achieve a particular outcome: bringing a tempered approach based on self-awareness on some occasions and implementing different approaches on others, drawing on strengths related as much to human understanding as to technical ability.

Key questions for you to ask yourself as you grow your strengths are:

- Which strengths have I built on in the last six months?
- Which strengths do I want to use more over the next six months?
- What are the hidden strengths I need to make more of?

Look after your strengths

A consistent message in challenging times is to be optimistic, energetic and enthusiastic while being rooted in realism. Confidence and optimism building on your strengths can lead to a self-fulfilling prophecy. Success is about

Drawing on your strengths means that even in the most challenging circumstances you can see opportunities.

being self-assured, with confidence having as much impact as capability. You have to believe in yourself as well as being honest about yourself. It enables you to believe that there is a solution, however tough the situation might seem. How you build on your strengths will give you a competitive advantage.

Building on your strengths means being positive and being objective. Optimism must not come across as denial. People who lose heart are those who have lost their positive belief that there can be a successful outcome. You have to believe that your strengths will mean that you can become part of the future and are not part of the problem. Growing your strengths can give you confidence that you can make choices, even in the most difficult circumstances.

➡️≫ Moving forward

➢ Be clear about what you think your strengths are.
➢ Seek the views of others on what your strengths are.
➢ Understand how your strengths have grown and developed over recent years.
➢ Be positive about how you can use your strengths in the future.
➢ Be clear what specific strengths you want to develop further over the next few months.

Chapter 2
Understand Your Least Strong Areas

Understanding and being honest about your least strong areas is crucial to making progress. Pretending that your least strong areas do not exist may work in the short term, but is folly in the long term. A range of different strategies can be applied, including working with others who can compensate for these relative weaknesses, choosing an area of focus that uses your strengths to the best possible effect and having clear strategies in place when you need to use your least strong areas. Giving yourself a reward when you do use your least strong areas to good effect can be a valuable way of reinforcing your capability.

Why is it important to understand your least strong areas?

You cannot always survive just by applying the competencies that you use well. Either a situation demands that you use an approach that is not your natural strength or others try to test you out in your least strong areas, be they customers, students, critics or your boss. A tennis player can always hold a racquet with their preferred hand, but a footballer who can only kick a ball with their right foot is not likely to be a major success at national level. For most of us, building up a basic competence in our non-preferred areas is unavoidable.

Develop your least strong areas

When I am coaching leaders, I often seek verbal feedback from their boss, peers and the staff reporting to them. I then summarise generic themes about strengths and areas to reflect on, which I feed back to the individual. Examples of areas to reflect on following verbal 360° feedback might include:

- Could you be clearer about the outcomes you want to see delivered?
- Could you sometimes be clearer what you want from people?
- How aware are you that you can sometimes come over as reluctant to make decisions?
- Is there a need to be more robust in tackling certain behaviours in others?
- Could more be done to enhance your visibility with particular groups of people?

I invite individuals to consider the areas to reflect on and decide where they want to take action or not. Sometimes they say they do not wish to change their approach, while on other issues they want to be clear on their next steps.

Sometimes what others regard as your least strong areas are not features that you want to change. While it is right to take account of the views of others, you are the best judge about whether you want to change in an area that others have reservations about; although if the comments are coming from your boss, there is a much greater incentive to adapt your approach! Where your staff are expressing reservations, careful discussion with them about why you take certain approaches can make a big difference and help you judge whether it is in fact necessary to change your approach.

Developing your least strong areas normally requires an action plan involving:

- Clarity about where you want to get to
- The steps you are going to take
- How you are going to get feedback from others on your progress
- Rewarding yourself when you achieve certain steps.

We all have feet of clay

You would not be the first person to feel least strong in certain areas. Kevin White, a highly experienced HR director, gives this advice:

Do not be taken in by the trappings of achievement. Everyone has feet of clay. Realise that it is natural to be uncomfortable and not confident. You do not need to be a different sort of person but better at the person you are. You need to ensure you have joy in your work to give you energy and the resilience to survive.

Helen was very conscious that she had a strong need for recognition. She was increasingly self-aware about the need to manage her own reactions in different circumstances. She was conscious that her need for recognition meant that she did not always react emotionally to a situation in the most appropriate way. Her reflections as she learnt to deal with situations were:

I am increasingly aware of the issues and I am probably more on top of them than I think. I need to be strongly focused. I often felt I needed to be 'invited' to discussions; now I will invite myself if I believe it is an issue to which I can add value.

Helen's experience illustrates how a vulnerability can be dealt with by being self-aware and:

- Looking at what has worked in the past to help reduce the issue.
- Believing that there is evidence that it can be overcome.
- Adopting a focused approach that enables effective progress to be made.
- Realising that it is not an issue that is going to get in the way in the long run.

In their book *Now, Discover Your Strengths*, Marcus Buckingham and Donald Clifton talk about a weakness as 'anything that gets in the way of excellent performance'. They discuss five creative strategies for managing a talent out of a weakness:

- *Get a little better at it*: this might not sound very ambitious, but in some instances it is the only workable strategy.
- *Design a support system*: which is about ensuring there are people around you who compliment your particular contribution.
- *Use one of your strongest themes*: to overwhelm your weakness.
- *Find a partner*: which is about teaming up with another individual to bring a complementary approach.
- *Just stop doing it*: which might be a strategy of last resort, but when it is used can be empowering.

Sometimes you can reframe what some regard as a weakness as a strength. For example, you may be criticised for delaying making a decision when in fact you are good at waiting for the right moment to be decisive. Some may see you as too soft-hearted when really you are building up the maximum amount of understanding about how people are reacting in a particular situation.

Is this about least strong areas or preferences?

It can be very helpful to use the language of preferences rather than least strong areas. For example, the MBTI® questionnaire (the Myers-Briggs Type Indicator® questionnaire is a leading personality and self-development tool) assesses preferences on four dimensions, each consisting of two opposite sides. The normal way to introduce the MBTI questionnaire is to talk about the concept of preferences and encourage people to write their signature first with their preferred hand and then with their non-preferred hand. The usual comment is that writing your signature with the preferred hand feels quick, is effortless and easy. Writing with the non-preferred hand can feel slow, awkward and unnatural but is possible. This exercise is a good way to illustrate the concept of preference.

The four dimensions used in the MBTI framework are set out in Box 2. They represent these key preferences:

- Where do you prefer to focus your attention and how are you energised?
- What kind of information do you prefer to pay attention to and how do you acquire information?
- How do you prefer to make decisions?
- Which lifestyle do you prefer in terms of coming to closure on decisions or keeping open to new experiences and information?

The MBTI approach encourages people to assess themselves into one particular, overall preference type, but there is also a clear emphasis on the individual recognising when they need to use each of the eight preferences. The results from the MBTI assessment process can lead to a constructive conversation about developing the preferences they use less often. The MBTI approach is often very valuable in enabling people to see how they have used their least strong preferences to good effect and how they could use them more effectively in the future.

Box 2   MBTI Preferences

The MBTI Dimensions: E-I (Extroversion – Introversion)

Where do you prefer to focus your attention?
How are you energised?

E Preference

Preference to draw your energy from the world around you, from 'doing', from involvement in external events and contact with people.

P Preference

Preference to draw your energy from your internal world, through quiet reflection, focusing on your inner thoughts or ideas.

The MBTI Dimensions: S-N (Sensing – Intuition)

What kind of information do you prefer to pay attention to? How do you acquire information?

S Preference

Preference for attending to specific information and facts to find out what is actually happening. Observant of what is going on around you and especially focused on the practical realities of a situation.

N Preference

Preference for attending to the patterns and associations between facts rather than the facts themselves. Interested in connections and looking for what might be rather than what is, focusing on ideas and possibilities.

The MBTI Dimensions: T-F (Thinking – Feeling)

How do you prefer to make decisions?

T Preference

Preference for making decisions from a detached standpoint, by analysing the logical consequences of a choice or action. Applying objective criteria and using consistent rules and principles. Often trying to stand outside a situation to examine it objectively and analyse cause and effect.

F Preference

Preference for making decisions from an involved standpoint, by gauging the impact of actions on your personal convictions. Seeking harmony and judging the importance of the different values involved. Often placing yourself inside a situation so as to identify personally with its key values.

The MBTI Dimensions: J-P (Judging – Perceiving)

Which lifestyle do you prefer?

J Preference

Preference for coming to closure on decisions, preferring to live life in scheduled and orderly ways and wanting things to be controlled and regulated. Liking to make plans and then sticking to those plans until they are completed. Getting satisfaction from getting things done.

P Preference

Preference for keeping open to new experiences and information. Preferring to live life in a flexible, spontaneous way. Comfortable going with the flow and taking advantage of last-minute options as they arise. Enjoying using resourcefulness and adaptability, and feeling constrained by plans and structures.

Recognise your least strong areas

Some people have reservations about using the language of weaknesses or least strong areas. While it is undermining to focus on weaknesses too much, an expert in any sphere is conscious of their least strong areas. Describing them as less developed preferences can be helpful, but it can also be a distortion of reality. When you are not good at doing something it is often better to be honest about it rather than describe it as a less developed preference.

Philippa was always focused on getting results. When she was told that her unrelenting focus was a source of considerable irritation to her colleagues, she was annoyed and resentful. It was her determination that had ensured good progress had been made in addressing difficult issues. She found it difficult to accept that her approach could be demeaning to others and sap their energy and resolve.

Eventually a colleague plucked up the courage to be frank with Philippa and quietly but firmly told her that she needed to modify her approach or lose people's goodwill even more. She protested that she was not very good at the 'people stuff' and was not convinced it was important in any case. Reluctantly, she agreed to work with a coach on how best to rebuild relationships with colleagues and find a new, more constructive way of working with them.

Philippa was never going to be a naturally empathetic person, but she began to work hard at building shared agendas. Gradually her reputation for demeaning others disappeared. Philippa still demonstrated a clear focus, but carried people with her more effectively now. She was grateful that a good colleague had been honest with her and encouraged her to develop a modified approach to working with colleagues.

Seek to grow in your least strong areas

When George did his self-assessment at the start of a coaching programme, he was clear that the areas where he wanted to grow and develop were about inner confidence, being able to speak authoritatively, acquiring more natural authority and developing the insight that comes with doing a job really well. He felt that he was always trying to catch up. He wanted to be ahead of the game and not behind it.

In terms of developing inner confidence, George reflected on occasions when his inner confidence had been there in one-to-one conversations and in crisis situations when quick decisions were needed and when logical decisions were being worked through. He said that his inner confidence was less good when competing issues were coming at him, when he was in a group full of people who had lots to say and in some fast-moving situations when he found it difficult to make an impact.

We talked about the importance of focusing on the positive aspects of a situation, as he tended to consider the negative aspects first. We talked about focusing on when the positive had worked successfully and having as his mantra the phrase 'Just do it', to help him overcome his reticence.

With a combination of these steps George found his inner confidence growing. There was new evidence that he could be confident in situations where he had previously felt unsure of himself. He made marked progress through a step-by-step approach, gradually overcoming what he perceived as a weakness. The result was much more effective contributions in a range of different types of meetings.

Observing yourself and laughing at yourself can provide a very good basis for becoming more relaxed about your strengths and areas that are less strong. Once you become more accepting and amused by your least strong areas, a transformation can begin. You can become more at one with yourself and more effective in contributing in situations where you previously felt much less at home.

➡≫ Moving forward

➣ Be honest about your least strong areas.
➣ Be clear how your preferences are changing over time.
➣ Do not disregard evidence of when you have used least strong areas or less developed preferences well.
➣ Build a group of friends and colleagues who complement your relative strengths.
➣ Celebrate when you use your least strong areas effectively.

Chapter 3
Embed Your Values

Your hidden or explicit values determine much of your behaviour. You may be reluctant to talk about your values, but all of us have guiding principles whether or not we care to admit it. It is by recognising your values, clarifying them and embedding them that you ensure you have maximum impact with minimum internal distress. Searching for consistency between values and behaviours is part of embedding wisdom. Ensuring that you come over in a consistent way will increase the likelihood of you being taken seriously by others.

Why is embedding values important?

Understanding your values and how they drive you is crucial to understanding why you react in particular ways. Understanding your motivations in different situations enables you to make the best possible contribution

The values that are important to you will be visible to those around you, whether you welcome that fact or not! in work or wider activities. Embedding your values provides a valuable moral compass for your decisions.

Recognise your values

Values are 'beliefs or behaviours which are of particular importance to an individual in the way they live their lives and interact with other people' (*The Four Vs of Leadership*, Capstone, 2006). Personal values result from beliefs about the right or wrong way of doing things. They are based on moral judgements (absolute or relative to the particular situations) and experience.

Key questions that are worth asking yourself are:

- What personal values drive me?
- How captive am I to my inherited values?
- How do my values cope with major external change?
- What is the interplay between individual and corporate values in the organisation in which I work?

Living your values can mean asking yourself honest questions about:

- What is keeping me going?
- Where do I believe I can make a difference?
- What behaviours are most important to me?
- What personal qualities do I most want to reinforce in myself and others?

Live your values

Those who make the biggest difference and generate the most respect often bring sharpness of thinking and clarity around values. They live out behaviours that build trust, confidence and partnership. Living your values in such a situation is not a soft diversion. It provides a foundation for building effective working relationships rooted in a shared belief about what will work and how partnership and collaboration will deliver effective outcomes.

To be convincing, values and principles have to come from inside you. Leaders who cope well in very challenging times make decisions based on clear principles, have a sense of conviction about the right thing to do **You cannot convincingly feign your values or borrow them.** and are able to balance short- and long-term values. When things start to go wrong, a strong sense of moral responsibility can be sustaining in finding a solution.

In 2008 we did a piece of research at Praesta Partners, seeking out leaders who had been through times of extended turbulence. It was clear that strong leaders:

- Maintain their core attitudes and their beliefs no matter how much pressure they come under.
- Tackle each new challenge clearly and calmly, leading from the front to inspire those around them.
- Know how to look after themselves to maintain stamina and well-being for a lengthy and often exhausting period.

A central message from the research was the importance of 'doing the right thing'. Focusing on doing what you believe to be 'the right thing' maintains your sense of personal integrity, self-worth and even accomplishment, no matter what the final outcome. What someone regards as right can come from their own values and experiences or from having considered the perspective of trusted advisers. In our research, we saw effective leaders addressing the following key questions and finding a dynamic balance between them:

- What is right for the organisation?
- What is right for the people who work in it?
- What is right for me as a leader?

Bring self-awareness about your values

Sometimes values can be a source of distortion. Is there something rigid about your cultural baggage that gets in the way? Your beliefs and emotions produce a powerful cocktail that can send you off on a particular perspective that you might later regard as absurd.

Emotions such as disappointment, resentment, anger or fear can distort your understanding. Such negative emotions can eat away at your objectivity. Fear can take away your ability to analyse a problem effectively. The resolution is to be utterly honest with yourself: to be clear what your values are and recognise the extent to which your behaviour patterns at times of stress divert you from your values. It is by applying this plumb line that you are able to see how your behaviour becomes distorted and what steps might be necessary to bring it back into line.

When you find yourself blaming others, this is often a good indication of the fact that you're avoiding the responsibility of taking action yourself. If there is a hint of blame, your values are at risk of being tarnished and the prospect of working together effectively as a team will go out of the window. Whatever your own or others' failings, thriving depends on accepting the reality of what has happened, being consistent with your values and not overlaying emotional blame, either on yourself or others.

Living your values is about putting any shocks or surprises into a wider context. Unexpected events may need you to expend immediate energy, but they need to be seen realistically as either a one-day distortion or a major event with long-term implications. You don't need to be fearful of such events but rather focus on the reality of what might happen. If you are clear on your guiding values, you are better able to achieve detachment and view setbacks as learning opportunities and not damaging defeats.

Know your values

I encourage people to write down their key values and what those values mean to them. This simple and quick exercise provides a good framework for discussion about where those values come from, how they influence your life and work and how you want to develop them further. Reflect quickly and articulate or write down the first thoughts you have about your values – this can be helpful in identifying what is most important. A more comprehensive approach might be to go through the following steps. Consider:

- What have been the strongest influences shaping my values? Is it family, culture, community, faith or education?

- What have been the strongest values resulting from these influences?
- What are the values that have been important for me?
- What are the four most important values in this list?

Look closely at each value, possibly spending spare moments during the day on one of the values, then going through the same process on a different day with another of the values, asking yourself the following questions:

- What does the value mean to me?
- How has the value been relevant to me in particular situations?
- Is the value standing the test of time or does it need to evolve?
- Are these four values robust enough for the future?
- Would those around me recognise me living these values?
- How would I hold myself to account for living these values?

Look through a list of possible values such as those set out in Box 3. You might then reflect on which four you resonate with most, or which you would like to reinforce in yourself.

You might conclude that some of your core values are absolutely right and are fundamental to your success, but you might also conclude that certain values need to be reinforced if you are going to raise your game successfully. For example, as you move into more senior roles, determination, partnership and foresight might become ever more important.

Box 3   Illustrative List of Possible Values

Trust	Integrity
Openness	Innovation
Honesty	Loyalty
Boldness	Companionship
Rigour	Security
Courage	Respect
Creativity	Order
Initiative	Partnership
Happiness	Passion
Persistence	Quality
Frankness	Fulfilment
Commitment	Purposefulness
Friendship	Self-control
Dependability	Joyfulness
Delivery	Stewardship
Service	Success
Fairness	Determination
Diversity	Encouragement
Justice	Character
Profitability	Responsiveness
Learning	Adventure
Clarity	Foresight
Sincerity	Compassion
Humour	Forgiveness
Adaptability	Cooperation
Recognition	Kindness
Resolve	Warmth
Conviction	Transparency
Single-mindedness	Professionalism

Part of living values effectively is demonstrating that you are interested in the people with whom you are working. James Caplin, in *I Hate Presentations* (Capstone, 2008) talks about too many presenters being stuck in the school-essay mindset of imparting information. This involves telling a long story about the past ('how we got here'), the present ('where are we now') and the future ('where we are going'). The 'gold nugget' in what Caplin is saying is the need to understand the difference between being interesting *to* an audience and being interested *in* them. He says, 'If you approach from the point of view of being interesting to the audience you will become little more than someone becoming an act. If, however, your audience senses you are interested in them, you are on your way to establishing a bond between you.'

At the core of living values effectively is demonstrating that you are interested in the people you are working with and the issues they are addressing.

Focusing on saying something interesting may not resonate and may fail to 'light a spark'. You are much more likely to ignite interest and energy when there is a sense of empathy, shared concerns and values.

Look after your values

Looking after your values is both a personal and a corporate responsibility. Within an organisation, there is a responsibility on individuals both to live the corporate values and to support others in doing the same. The best organisations clearly articulate their vision and values and what these mean for different people. This provides an effective benchmark against which individuals can assess what behaviours are appropriate and what will be the consequence of living those values. A good example of an articulation of vision and values, and what it means for staff, customers and delivery partners has recently been published by the UK Department for Communities and Local Government (Box 4). This provides a clear framework for making decisions.

Box 4 Department of Communities and Local Government

Our Vision

Creating great places where people want to live, work and raise a family

Our Values

We are ambitious and creative	We act openly and as one department	We give people the chance to shine	We give people a voice

What It Means for Our Staff

We focus on delivering effectively, stretching ourselves, exceeding people's expectations, and always looking for ways to lift our game.	We work well together. Our communications and actions are open, honest and straightforward, and we listen to what others have to say.	We respect and value individuals, unlock and develop their talents, give them the opportunity to grow, take responsibility, and celebrate and reward their contributions.	We welcome questions and ideas, and we respect everyone's contributions. We challenge and respond well to challenge.

Box 4   *Continued*

What It Means for People and Communities

Improving places and communities, using money wisely and where it can make the greatest difference.

We welcome people's views and work with them to make communities stronger and more cohesive.

Individuals and communities are treated with respect and are given opportunities to contribute to our work.

We empower people and communities to speak out and shape their neighbourhoods.

What It Means for Delivery Partners

We forge strong partnerships built on a shared vision and what works best in practice.

We work with partners so that together we deliver the greatest possible benefits. Our partners can trust what we say and do.

We respect and value everyone we work with. We give partners the chance to show the best that they can do – for those we all serve.

We give responsibility for delivering to those best able to make the biggest difference.

Another excellent example is the recently adopted mission, values and delivery outcomes of West Mercia Police (Box 5). These were agreed following an extensive internal consultation process that was aimed at securing significant levels of staff 'buy-in'. The use of the 'I' word puts a strong focus on individuals living the values and using them as they continue to raise their game.

Box 5   West Mercia Police

Our Mission

Serving – Protecting – Making the Difference

Our Values

I act with honesty, fairness and respect in serving our communities and the people within them.	I take pride in working within an organisation dedicated to protecting people and upholding the law.	I always take responsibility; my contribution makes a valued difference.

Successful Delivery of Our Mission Between Now and 2012 Will Result in the Following Outcomes:

The public have confidence in us and express satisfaction with our policing service.	Levels of crime and anti-social behaviour remain low.	Our communities feel safe.

At the centre of looking after your values is building trust. Trust gets people energised and is essential to the sound health of an organisation. Focusing on building trust can have a powerful influence for good in enabling individuals in an organisation to live both personal and organisational values effectively. Box 6 sets out a very helpful perspective from Sally Bibb and Jeremy Koudri in their book *Trust Matters* (Palgrave Macmillan, 2004).

Box 6   Leaders Who Focus on the Value of Building Trust

❖ Have insight into themselves.
❖ Create an atmosphere of expectation and trust, and take responsibility.
❖ Have clear intent and are honest, without hidden agendas.
❖ Have the organisation's and employees' best interests at heart.
❖ Have credibility, are consistent and trust others.
❖ Let others see their passion – it is obvious what they care about.
❖ Speak from the heart, not just from the intellect.
❖ Confront   people   without   being confrontational.
❖ Do not mind admitting they do not know.
❖ Have integrity and use power positively.

From Sally Bibb and Jeremy Koudri (2004) *Trust Matters: For Organisational and Personal Success*, London: Palgrave Macmillan.

Moving forward

➢ Be clear what your values are.
➢ Understand how your values have influenced your behaviour in the past.
➢ Articulate to yourself how your values are going to enable you to raise your game in the near future.
➢ Be clear about the relationship between your values and those of the organisation of which you are part.
➢ Reflect on the extent to which demonstrating you are interested in others and building trust in your relationship with others are evidence about how you live your values.

Chapter 4
Create an Equilibrium

Creating an equilibrium in yourself involves looking at the way you use your time and energy. It means that you use up less energy doing difficult things and you are better able to withstand problems that come at you from unexpected directions. Your personal equilibrium needs to accommodate the ebbs and flows of life and the patterns of living that work best for you. An equilibrium that ties in with your values increases the likelihood of your being at peace with yourself. It also helps bring you an optimism rooted in practical reality rather than one permanently swayed by your emotional condition.

Why is creating an equilibrium important?

There are patterns in so many aspects of life. Your patterns of sleeping, eating and exercise determine your physical well-being. Your intellectual well-being comes from using your brain on a regular basis. Your emotional well-being flows from your understanding of yourself and your ability to communicate emotions effectively with others. Your spiritual well-being results from knowing what matters most in your life so that you keep things in perspective, whether this comes from enduring interests or relationships or is rooted in beliefs and faith. The rhythms of living that underpin this equilibrium need to be flexible, but if they are disrupted on a regular basis your well-being will suffer and your effectiveness will diminish.

Recognise what holds you in equilibrium

James is very clear what helps hold him in equilibrium. For him, it comes from being in the centre of an organisation, having direct access to a very good boss, the sense of challenge that comes from being asked to do interesting things, a sense of achievement in having done them well, and wider interests outside the office. His equilibrium is a combination of the context he is in and his own frame of mind.

He is conscious that when he does not sense that he is in equilibrium, he begins to be negative and to experience a downward spiral that saps his confidence and energy. It has the effect of making him feel as if he is looking out through dark glasses. We talked about different approaches to tackling this downward spiral, which included moving to a different location, developing a thicker skin and challenging any sense of feeling 'I am crap'.

We talked about self-criticism, self-doubt and self-deprecation, all of which disrupt our equilibrium. The next steps for James in getting the right equilibrium involved investing in personal relationships, continually seeking new challenges, never underestimating what he had achieved and recognising and enjoying what he delivers. We reflected on the consequences of the anxiety that comes when he is out of equilibrium, which can lead to paralysis, negative thoughts, an experience of being overwhelmed and feelings of inadequacy. There can be a sense of 'I am drowning and I cannot cope'.

The challenge is how to learn and grow from a sense of anxiety, how to get the adrenalin flowing so that the anxiety works in your favour and not against you. One approach that James and I discussed was naming that sense of anxiety and acknowledging that it is a phase that, on all past evidence, will last for a limited period. We discussed coping strategies such as laughing at yourself, recognising and trying to box anxiety, and trying to keep anxiety under control through remembering stories that have helped him move through it in the past. We talked through key phrases to help James keep a sense of equilibrium:

- I will always do things with a smile on my face.
- The touch of anxiety is good because it keeps me on my toes.
- I keep wanting to take on challenges because I enjoy them.

Retain your perspective

Recognising when you are in or out of equilibrium is central to understanding yourself and retaining your perspective. Keeping track of perspective and scale is crucial.

Is this a drama or a crisis? Is it just apprehension or is it reality? As well as trying to understand the connections between different current events, it is important to understand the connections between the present and the future and to distinguish what matters most and what is less important.

Success comes from maintaining a sense of purpose and independence and refusing to be defined by any particular crisis or problem. It is about depersonalising events to keep objectivity and a long-term sense of perspective. It may not always mean accepting what people say at face value. It may mean pushing back to find the best equilibrium.

Clarify the right equilibrium in different roles

Sometimes we can get the point of equilibrium wrong. Bernard, a regional director in a government organisation, arrived in his job thinking that he could single-mindedly make a big difference. He was outspoken about the lack of information and the top-heaviness of the organisation. He acknowledged in retrospect that he came at it like a bull at a gate and got everybody's back up. He subsequently approached his role in a very different way and considered the effects of what he said on other people. He moderated his tone and language and saw things in a new way. Now he does not feel that he has to win every battle, he thinks thoughtfully and carefully before each engagement and he is now making a major difference in the organisation.

For Bernard, raising his game meant finding a different equilibrium that was more appropriate to the organisation of which he was now part. He found that his new approach meant there was a new resonance between his style and what was appreciated in the organisation. There are times when equilibrium becomes too cosy and the resultant complacency inhibits progress. Discordance is needed and old rhythms need to be broken. But when they are disrupted, this needs to be done for a purpose and with the intent of moving towards a new equilibrium.

Building effective equilibrium can require action at a number of different levels. It is a balance between the short-term and the long-term; between the extent to which you are guided by past experience and future experimentation; and between following your preferred approach and adopting approaches suggested by others.

It can also be about finding the most creative way of using your time and energy; developing your listening skills and handling emails well, for instance. Practical suggestions on increasing your listening skills are set out in Box 7 and on handling emails well in Box 8.

Often the most effective way of keeping in equilibrium is to do the basics well.

Look after your equilibrium

Successful leaders are able to create a pattern of equilibrium in interrelated areas. Six key areas that matter most when building your equilibrium are:

Box 7   Developing your listening skills

- ❖ Value the people you are listening to.
- ❖ Ask open questions.
- ❖ Listen to learn and discern.
- ❖ Be fully engaged and give your sole undivided attention.
- ❖ Bring objectivity.
- ❖ Show you are enlivened by what you hear.
- ❖ Be willing to be surprised.
- ❖ Create a sense that you are walking alongside the other person.
- ❖ Accept that your qualities can enable the other person to have their own insights. You do not have to know all the answers.

From *Conversation Matters* by Peter Shaw (Continuum, 2005).

- *Rigour*, which is about focus and determination, not letting go when obstacles are put in your way. It is about having a framework that is robust and tested. It is about attending sequentially to specific issues and being rigorous in reaching conclusions in the time available.
- *Resilience*, which is about coping with the buffeting that comes with decision making in a faster world. It involves holding firm to principles and values when all around you seem to be losing theirs.
- *Relationship*, which is the ability to build alliances and persuade people of a particular course of action. Effective relationships that work are at the heart of

---

Box 8   Handling emails well

Reading Them

❖ Do not feel that you have to read each email when it arrives.
❖ Focus the time when you read emails.
❖ Delete them as soon as you have dealt with them.
❖ Give yourself time to reflect when an instant judgement might be counter-productive.
❖ Understand the emotional baggage that might be part of the tone of an email.

Sending Them

❖ Only use 'reply all' when that is essential.
❖ Save a draft of a critical email and reflect on it before sending it.
❖ Speak in preference to emailing.
❖ Think through how recipients are likely to respond to your message.
❖ Send regular notes of encouragement.

---

everything we do. Success only comes when others are persuaded.

• *Responsiveness*, which is the balance between clarity of principle and values and responding flexibly to different perspectives and external changes. It is being responsive and being seen to be responsive using effective communication (listening, engaging, influencing and persuading).

- *Relaxation*, which is a balance between engaging in activities that sap energy and performing those that give energy. It is about using energy in the most effective way, allowing bursts of energy when they are most needed.
- *Responsibility*, which involves clarity about individual responsibilities and knowing where the boundaries are. It is not feeling the responsibility of the whole world on your shoulders, but knowing what you are responsible for.

If you can keep these six areas in reasonable balance, you are more likely to find an equilibrium that will enable you to cope with the changes that affect you.

Know your rhythms

What rhythms are most important to you and how can you adapt them as circumstances change? You need rhythms that are flexible enough to cope with unavoidable external factors and are consistent enough to keep you at your best in terms of your physical, intellectual, emotional and spiritual well-being.

Looking after your rhythms is principally about understanding them, nurturing them and building a sense of resilience within them. If they become too rigid, they become like a brittle pot that is easily smashed into small pieces. If your rhythms are like a well-crafted pot they can cope with liquids of different temperatures and are unlikely to break unless dropped from a considerable height!

Use phrases or mantras that help you maintain your rhythms. They could be texts or phrases from your faith or lines from poetry. They could be phrases like 'It will be alright on the night'. Even the most trivial of phrases can help in keeping your cool and your rhythms when the going gets tough.

 ## Moving forward

➤ Recognise what sort of equilibrium works best for you.
➤ Build an equilibrium that takes account of your work and personal responsibilities.
➤ Continue to develop your listening skills.
➤ Recognise when your rhythms are in danger of becoming brittle.
➤ Be clear how you build energy into the different aspects of your life.

Section B
First Steps

This section is about initial steps that are needed as you begin to raise your game. Here we will look at how to:

- *Address your self-doubts and your fears*
- *Believe that you can do difficult things*
- *Know who your supporters and stakeholders are*
- *Take some risks*

Imagine you are setting out on a long walk. You are apprehensive and not sure about your capabilities. You want to know who your companions are going to be. You recognise that you are going to have to be adventurous and take some risks. You are ready to put your best foot forward and stride out, recognising that the journey will not be straightforward.

Section 8
First Steps

Chapter 5
Address Your Self-Doubt and Your Fears

Living with self-doubt and fears is part of life. The strength of your self-doubt will rise and fall and bringing fears under reasonable control is not always straightforward. Rubbing along, living with your self-doubt and fears is a fact of life, but sometimes you can contain and even befriend your fears. If you are to step up successfully it is important that you recognise and understand your doubts and fears. Sometimes you just have to learn to live with them. Your fears may well diminish over time and it is possible to reach an equilibrium where your fears do not get in the way of whatever success is important to you.

Why is understanding self-doubt and your fears important?

If you do not understand your self-doubt and fears, your behaviour can be distorted. You can reach a road block to your progress that stops you getting anywhere near achieving your full potential. Understanding your self-doubt and fears can be a painful process as it means being utterly honest with yourself and facing up to the action you need to take.

Living with self-doubt

Self-doubt is something many of us just have to live with, but it can give us useful messages and can diminish its impact over time. Finlay Scott, chief executive of the General Medical Council, talks about the combination of self-doubt and self-belief. He says:

> *Self-doubt can haunt you. You need the confidence to lead in difficult situations and the recognition that most of what you do is right. But self-doubt does have the benefit of leading you to drive to do better and to take precautions against things going wrong. It means you can see the weaknesses and the risks, and are aware of needing to see the consequences of decisions. Self-doubt does not need to paralyse, it can be a valuable tool.*

The fear of failure can be a powerful force for good or for ill. It can drain you of energy and whittle away your enthusiasm and optimism. It can drive you to solve problems and ensure that you take the steps that are necessary to ensure success.

There can often be a difference between your outer world of confidence and your inner world of doubt or vulnerability. Being honest about your vulnerabilities provides an essential starting point for moving on. What practical steps can you take to get your fears and vulnerabilities into proportion? These might include:

- Talking to close family members.
- Sharing your fears with close friends.
- Doing something different like walking, swimming or reading a novel.
- Moving completely away from the context that causes the fear.
- Being deliberately in the place that causes the fear and seeing how you best control it.
- Thinking of those whose fear is far more acute than your own.

Recognise your fears

Fear can be a good thing, up to a point! Fear can create a rush of adrenalin, which gives you the energy to get out of a difficult situation. If there were no fear you could end up making rash decisions, insensitive to the likely reactions of others. On the other hand, fear can also produce a damaging paralysis that inhibits progress into a more secure position.

It can be helpful to be frank about the fears that worry you most. Write them down and then score them on a scale of one to ten, where one is illusory and ten is highly likely. Then you can ask yourself:

- When is each fear at its worst?
- What are the warning signs that this fear might burst out?
- What in the past has reduced the size of the fear?

Understanding your fears better

Addressing your fears is not about ignoring them, it is about defining them and understanding them. Looking at fear from a variety of angles can help you to understand it and contain it.

If you wake up afraid at 4 a.m.:

- Be explicit about what the fear is.
- Perhaps write it down, with three reasons for the fear being there.
- Note down three ways in which the fear could be addressed.
- Identify three reasons it is not as acute as it might at first appear.

Later in the day, take another look at the notes you made:

- Are the reasons for the fear still there?
- Has the fear increased or diminished throughout the day?
- Have you been able to apply any of the ways to address the fear?
- Are there practical steps you can take to reduce the fear further?

Fear can be seriously overrated. Most of our worst fears never happen. In his book *The Gathering Storm* (Penguin,

2005), Winston Churchill wrote about the early days of the Second World War:

When I look back on all these worries, I remember the story of the old man who said on his death bed that he had had a lot of trouble in his life, most of which had never happened.

Moving on from self-doubt or fears

Henry has a tendency to imagine dire consequences arising out of problems, real or perceived, in his working life. This imagining of dire consequences causes mental anguish, meaning it is harder to concentrate on other things. He sometimes 'catastrophises', whereby small incidents can be built up into potential major crises. For example, a document that has been mislaid is immediately regarded as likely to be in the hands of a critical journalist, when it is most likely to have got mixed up with other papers. In Henry's office a comment to a colleague becomes viewed as a remark that could be misconstrued and likely to lead to a breakdown in their relationship. The one small mistake is pictured as likely to lead to the end of a career.

Practical steps that work for Henry in these circumstances include:

- Writing out the line to take if he is challenged.
- Sharing the problem and talking it through with a third party.
- Getting the timetable clear about next steps and trying to control it.
- Focusing on what he needs to do now and not being distracted.

Henry talks about the increased level of self-awareness that comes from acknowledging his emotional reactions; even if he cannot stop 'catastrophising', it helps to know that this is what he is doing. His strategy is a combination of observing himself and being conscious of when the trigger point might happen, coupled with going for long walks at the weekend and taking regular exercise. When there is a growing sense of making a mountain out of a molehill, Henry has learned the art of deep breathing, whether sitting still or standing upright. His key questions to himself are:

- Am I doing the things I can control?
- Am I pacing things right, involving people who can help but resisting the temptation to tell everyone near me what I am worrying about?
- Is there a mantra I can use, such as 'Do what you can and then park the issue and focus hard on the next thing'?

During challenging times, it can be hard to admit what you cannot do; this can feel like an admission of failure. However, the ability to be honest with yourself is a considerable leadership strength. Central to this is recognising when you may be about to 'lose it'. Powerful emotions like disappointment, resentment, exhaustion, anger or fear can fundamentally affect your ability to do things logically or to act rationally. If fears lead you to feel you are closing down, lacking confidence or blaming others, then remember these key steps:

- *Acknowledge* your problem: be honest with yourself that you are in danger of becoming emotionally overwhelmed and accept that it is affecting your judgement and behaviour.

- *Evaluate* the impact: assess the importance of the situation and how your reaction is affecting your work and the people around you.
- *Step away*: take a break from the situation, however short. This can mean walking around the block and having a coffee, or deciding to delegate a task to someone else.

Keeping clarity about your self-doubt and your fears

Deal with reality and face the issues. Blanking your fears may mean that you have tunnel vision. While a clear focus is crucial, tunnel vision can mean that you do not understand where colleagues and stakeholders are coming from and do not reflect enough on who you should be talking to and listening to. You achieve clarity by getting a balance between articulating, listening and being available. Remember to give yourself space and time to reflect. Whatever your self-doubts or fears in a particular situation, you must strive to remain objective and try to make sure that your information is good enough to support the decisions you make. Triangulating your perspective with the views of trusted others is one of the most effective ways of keeping your fears in reasonable proportion.

Living with your fears may mean having a clear mantra such as 'Face the week and make the most of it' or 'I do not do failures: I am not going to fail'. Another approach is to befriend your fears and regard them as an ally. When the gremlin on your left shoulder whispers that you are inadequate or doomed to failure, maybe you can thank it for providing a warning of potential problems or box it in so that its undermining effect can be restrained. Humouring the gremlin and trying to laugh at its ridiculous suggestions can create an inner dialogue that is much less damaging than you might have feared.

There is a fascinating inter-relationship between love and fear. The Apostle John wrote, 'There is no fear in love. Perfect love drives out fear.' Perhaps the best antidote to fear is a combination of the bonds of love shared with family and friends, companionship with trusted colleagues and the support that comes through mentoring or coaching relationships.

A key step in raising your game is to reach equilibrium with your self-doubts and your fears. This is not about dismissing them completely, it is about recognising that they exist and living with them. It is having practical steps to take when a situation feels scary. Box 9, on the following page sets out some illustrative steps to take when a problem feels scary.

➡️≫ Moving forward

➢ Try to understand the causes of self-doubt or fear.
➢ Try to be as rational as possible in the way you respond to fear.
➢ Remember that many doubts and fears are illusory.
➢ Try to see the benefits that flow from your fears.
➢ Be clear how you best keep your doubts and fears under reasonable control so that they do not disrupt your equilibrium.

Box 9   What to Do When Tackling A Problem Feels Scary

❖ How have you tackled this sort of problem successfully in the past?
❖ What are the components of the problem and which of them might be causing you the fear?
❖ How might you get more information in order to reduce the level of uncertainty?
❖ Can you write down what specific factors are causing you to feel fearful?
❖ Can you seek the views of others on how significant the problems are?
❖ What practical steps might you take to reduce the level of uncertainty?
❖ How might you build support from others for the steps that need to be taken?
❖ What would you advise somebody else to do if they were feeling scared in a similar situation?
❖ What are your three practical steps?
❖ What would make you laugh in this situation?

Chapter 6
Believe You Can Do Difficult Things

Believing you can do difficult things is at the heart of raising your game. This is not self-belief based on an inflated sense of your own self-importance, it is self-belief rooted in your competence, self-worth and values. Self-belief comes from recognising your own qualities and acknowledging the contribution you are making to the world, either by virtue of the expectations of others or by a more private, inner conviction arising from personal affirmation or faith. Honing your ability to do difficult things perpetuates a growth in self-confidence and effectiveness.

Why is believing you can do difficult things important?

Very few of us can stand still for long. We end up going either forwards or backwards. If we think we have 'arrived' and don't need to do difficult things any longer, the likelihood is that we will decline in confidence and effectiveness. Sometimes doing difficult

Continuing to strive to do difficult things keeps us alert and growing in effectiveness.

things actually involves doing things you have done before but, perhaps because of health constraints, what was previously easy has now become difficult. Believing that difficult things can be done in these circumstances is just as important as when you are healthy. Believing you can do difficult things is not about trying to do the impossible, but continually stretching the boundaries so that one step after another you are reaching outcomes that have never felt possible before.

Collect the evidence

Kevin White, who has been HR director for two major UK government departments, talks about a person who demonstrated they had stepped up successfully by being able to perform and take others with them. This person was comfortable around the meeting table and a confident contributor in team meetings, showing passion in what he was doing and rising well to a challenge. When faced with new things, he set about doing them without embarrassment; he did not need to pretend he already knew it all or was doing a bigger job.

He was not pretending to be fully effective from day one. He was bringing a step-by-step approach and demonstrating that the job could be done without anguish. This impressed his director.

To Kevin, those who step up successfully are those who have an inner self-belief that allows them to blossom and demonstrate confidence. They do not feel false or come over that way. Their inner belief might come from their parents, their upbringing or their experience and is evident in a calm, confident approach. Kevin finds it dispiriting observing people who do not quite succeed because something is holding them back from moving on confidently; he wants to shake them up and make them realise that they can do it. But he accepts that tackling self-belief is not always that straightforward.

One way of building up your confidence to is to look back on the difficult things that you have accomplished. People all too rarely take the opportunity to take stock and celebrate things they have done that have gone well.

When Rosemary took stock about her progress as a senior manager over the preceding 18 months, she said:

I have done things I did not know I could do. I have learned how to build relationships that enable me to go forward successfully. I have learned how to motivate people to get things done successfully and that I need to rely on other people and not try and do everything myself. I am conscious how seriously people take my words and have become more deliberative as a consequence, and I have always believed in telling the truth and speaking my mind; in the long run that has always proved the right thing to do.

Can you reflect on your journey over the last 18 months in terms of how you have handled difficult tasks?

- When have you done difficult things well?
- What enabled you to be successful?
- Was there a point when you believed you could be successful?
- How did other people help you believe in yourself?
- How did you know that you were taking the right first steps?
- How did you assess whether you were making effective progress?

An honest affirmation of the resources and skills you have used successfully to do difficult things well can provide a firm basis for tackling other difficult tasks well in the future. False modesty can get in the way of building on what you have done successfully in the past.

Wear the badge

What you are called can have a powerful effect. Finlay Scott talks about a time when he was in the Territorial Army and was helping to support an indoor exercise at the Staff College, which required regular officers to role-play more senior roles to the one they currently held (Majors became Major Generals and others Brigadiers). The effect was immediate – the regular officers began to behave as if they were in the senior role straight away. When people wear a badge they often grow into the role.

When some individuals take on a more senior role there is virtually no period of transition. What enables that to happen? What do they do differently?

For some, wearing the 'badge' is comfortable immediately. For others, there is a degree of discomfort at the start and the ease of wearing the badge only comes gradually. Sometimes you need to allow yourself the pleasure of being given the badge to enable you to move up a step and to banish embarrassment.

Archie Hughes has held senior positions in both the private and public sector in aeronautical engineering. When he was 29 he did his first major job in the aeroplane business. He said that when you look above you, all you can see is the bottom of the floor above. He worked 14 hours a day to understand the four walls and the ceiling of the space he occupied.

For Archie, progress came through being confident in the contribution that he could make:

> *Do not try to be all things to all people. I had to trust my judgement in people. You cannot fool them when you are new to a role. It is taking their skills and using them well. It is understanding your own skills. I had to unlock people's potential. Often it was doing little things well first.*

The starting point in believing that you can do different things is acknowledging that other people think that you can do difficult things well. Every time you change jobs, somebody is choosing you. Someone has faith in you and is giving you a chance. They want you to succeed to justify their own selection.

Tackle difficult things with confidence

Difficult tasks tend to become less daunting when you have thought them through. Once a problem has been broken down into a sequence of steps, the outcome seems much more attainable. Writing a book of 40 000 words seems daunting and almost impossible; writing 25 separate chapters each of 1600 words seems far more attainable.

What might be the key elements of a personal strategy aimed at increasing your level of confidence in doing difficult things well?

■▶ ≫ Moving forward

➢ Celebrate what you have done well in the past.
➢ Try to see difficult things as an opportunity and not a threat.
➢ Break a difficult task down into a sequence of steps.
➢ Ensure that you have the best possible wise counsel around you.
➢ Be willing to use a mantra like 'Just do it'.

Chapter 7
Know Who Your Supporters and Stakeholders Are

Y ou can achieve very little on your own. You may think that you know the answer to a problem or that you have a unique contribution to bring; you may see yourself as the only person bringing detached wisdom when all around you seem to be bringing an unrealistic perspective; but to be successful you need to build supporters: a

**combination of bosses who will sponsor you, col-
leagues who will support you and followers who
will respond to the lead you give. Building supporters is about building trust and a shared agenda so
that there is a win/win in the delivery of outcomes
for everyone.**

Why is it important to know who your supporters are?

It is easier to see the enemy in front than your supporters
behind. Building a common purpose and a shared agenda
will mean that you are less likely to be stabbed in the
back. When you are working effectively with others the
overall effect of the creativity and the shared energy
is more than the sum of the parts. As you grow a team
of supporters you are building both allies when addressing current issues, and long-term backing for future
occasions.

Build an effective relationship with your boss

Hazel had just begun to work with the new chairperson
of her organisation. We talked about how she wanted to
come over in her conversations with this person. She
wanted to be seen as confident, clear and competent and
to be viewed as somebody the chair was comfortable with
and could rely on. We talked about what evidence the
chair would have over the next few weeks to see her like
this. Our conclusions were centred on the value of preparing for meetings with the chair and being both confident
and relaxed in those discussions. It was important that

the boss thought it was worthwhile to spend time talking to Hazel and also enjoyed being in her company. The key words confident, clear and competent helped Hazel centre herself as she prepared to meet the chair, and then assessing herself following the discussion. They provided the right balance between bringing intellectual clarity to the discussions and maintaining a sense of warmth and reliability.

As you approach a meeting with your boss, might the following be a useful checklist?

- What would be a successful outcome for the meeting?
- How might you best prepare for the meeting?
- If you were sat in the boss's shoes, what are the outcomes you would want from the meeting?
- What is the initial impact that you want to have on the boss as you walk in the room?
- How do you want to pace the meeting, if you have an opportunity to do so?
- How will you keep flexible to respond to the boss's mood?
- How would you like to try to ensure that you get clear conclusions from the meeting?
- How will you ensure that you keep up a relaxed and yet purposeful tone throughout the meeting?

Building effective relationships with key colleagues

Investing time in colleagues almost always pays dividends. This can be a combination of both formal and informal contact. The ideal is to create a situation where the hallmark of the relationship with another individual is that you are both committed to each other's success. Create situations that are win/win with your colleagues.

Building a relationship of trust is central to success.

Often, however, that is easier said than done when there are competing priorities. Sometimes there is no option but to risk making yourself unpopular when you are clear that a compromise outcome will create more problems than it solves.

Often it is worth systematically identifying the key people you need to get on your side to ensure success, and then to plan how you are going to inter-relate with them. It helps if you like the people concerned, but the preparation is particularly important if you feel a sense of unease with some individuals.

Make a list of who your supporters are:

- Identify the 6–10 people who will have a particular influence on your success.
- Assess the quality of your current relationship with them on a scale of 1–10, where 1 is poor and 10 is excellent.
- Identify what type of support you would like from each individual.
- Identify how you can support each individual.
- Reflect on the best way of building the strength of mutual support. (This could be through formal discussions, meetings or informal conversations.)
- Decide on your next steps in building the relationship and developing the support.
- Identify specific tasks where you can reinforce and develop your links with these individuals.

The danger with the list above is that it sounds very transactional. The best working relationships may be rooted in honest self-interest or mutual interest, but if trust, empathy and values are shared, the strength of mutual support is likely to be more long-lasting. The risk when there are strong emotional bonds is that objectivity can go out of the window. While short-term emotional rapport is fine, long-term supporters will bring intellectual objectivity as well as respect for an individual's personal strengths.

Building supporters among your staff

Building support is often about asking the right questions. Someone who feels that you have opened up new opportunities and avenues through your questioning and have enhanced their ability to solve their own problems will long remember you as an influential and treasured boss.

Practical steps for building supporters among your staff:

- Explicitly recognise the contribution of individuals.
- Identify teams that have made a distinctive contribution.
- Allocate time to mentor individual staff.
- Promote learning sets and set aside time to make a contribution to them.
- Take an interest in the personal development of individuals.
- Explain why you have taken forward particular actions.

- Be open about your learning journey.
- Give general praise and focused practical feedback, always checking how it is being received.

Building a network

Building a network of supporters frequently pays dividends. But how do you know where and how to invest your time in doing this? Building a wide number of semi-acquaintances hardly seems worth the effort. One of the joys of having a conversation is to try to find a common interest and resonance, so that two people can look at an issue in similar ways, or in ways that complement each other.

Building and keeping contacts in different spheres can seem self-serving or a waste of time. So much depends on what your motive is: if it is merely self-interest, then other people will realise this. If it is finding shared agendas and building mutual interests, then what might have initially appeared trans-actional can become both engaging and productive.

Good networking is not about platitudes, it is about using short conversations to the best possible effect and finding common ground.

When I was learning to use the Myers-Briggs Type Indicator, there was one other person on the course with the same overall preference set as me (ENTJ). A shared fascination with what the preference type might mean led to worthwhile conversations and a valuable new network.

It is right to guard against excessive and indulgent superficial networking, which may be very hearty but is of little consequence. It can soak up far too much time unless used in a thoughtful and realistic way. Not every contact leads to new revelations, but progress comes through enjoying engagement with a variety of people, finding those with whom you have a common bond and then building on that rapport.

From his leadership roles in public and private ventures in the aeronautical industry, Archie Hughes comments:

> *It is important to build a network quickly with customers and suppliers. You have to be known. Spend time building networks. It may not be immediately apparent what the value is for your existing role, but networking is never wasted. Business is a relationship game. Build networks for the future and do not lose sight of the people you leave behind.*

Communicate effectively with your supporters and stakeholders

Effective communication is about clarity, curiosity, thinking through consequences and being corporate.

- *Clarity:* This is about effective preparation, identifying key points, keeping it simple and then giving a message that is not too cluttered. It is ensuring that you are not diverted by the irrelevant.
- *Curiosity:* This is about listening hard and wearing the shoes of the people you are talking to, trying to understand where they are coming from and what their concerns and priorities are. Curiosity is also about looking around corners to try to find a way through problems.

- *Consequences:* This is about looking beyond the short-term to what might be the long-term benefits of different shared agendas or alliances.
- *Corporate:* This is about seeking shared success. It is being willing to engage in viewing an issue from different perspectives and finding a way forward that reinforces the shared agenda.

➡️≫ Moving forward

➢ Who will have the same view as you about what success is, and can you build a strong alliance with them?

➢ Who have been your supporters so far, and can you explicitly thank them for their support?

➢ Who are the 6–10 people whose support you would like to build, and how are you going to do that?

➢ What networks would you like to develop, and how will you ensure that you spend the right amount of time on this?

➢ How will you ensure that you maintain effective communication with your supporters?

Chapter 8
Take Some Risks

Part of raising your game successfully is being willing to take risks. This is not about foolhardy madness, it is about stretching your boundaries, widening your repertoire and being willing to be courageous. It is learning from what goes well and what goes less well. The wisdom that comes through experience is about being willing to take risks, learning from them and embedding the lessons that come from taking measured risks well.

Why is it important to take some risks?

Unless you take risks you will never know the extent of your capabilities. It is being willing to take risks that will stretch those capabilities. High jumpers can stay jumping over the height they are comfortable with, but most will want to try one notch higher. In training, they are further refining their run-up and their technique as they throw themselves over the bar. High jumpers know that if they take reckless risks in their run-up or trajectory, they have no hope of reaching a personal best height. Success for an athlete is a combination of precision in training and preparation, combined with that willingness to stretch the boundary one step further.

What sort of risks are you prepared to take?

Many of us do not want to risk failure or humiliation. The embarrassment of failure in front of our friends or peers can be devastating. Part of the answer lies in reframing what failure means. Viewed from a half empty perspective, failure is depressing and embarrassing. Viewed from a half full perspective, failure can be a learning experience from which you can take practical lessons to build into the next attempt.

Many of us can remember feeling humiliated in front of contemporaries at school. What helped then was encouragement from friends and parents. As adults we can suffer the same vulnerabilities. Remember, you still have people around you who will support and uphold you when you are falling on hard times.

Taking risks can sound a dangerous pastime. You shouldn't take risks when you're driving a car, for example. You don't take risks when you have inadequate preparation or foolhardy judgement. You must be clear about the outcomes you want to achieve; careful in identifying the opportunities and risks; and honest about your experience and abilities in dealing with a particular issue. Good risk assessment also means recognising the contribution that others make, assessing the probability of success, and being clear what the consequences are if the outcomes are not as desired.

Taking measured risks might involve applying an approach that has worked successfully in one situation to another (e.g. a presentation you had given has worked with one group and you would now like to try it with another). Other examples include asking another person to take the lead on a particular issue where you have taken the lead in the past; going outside your comfort zone in terms of speaking with a particular customers or partners with whom you have had limited previous dealings; or being willing to have difficult conversation about a subject that you have avoided in the past.

I encourage you to reflect on these questions:

- When do you stay in your comfort zone and show great reluctance in moving outside it?
- In what areas could you stretch the boundaries in terms of using your capabilities in new and different ways?
- Who are the best people to encourage you to take some calculated risks?
- Who will best support you if things go wrong?
- How can you prepare yourself effectively to be willing to take some risks?

How do you respond to risks?

Judith Macgregor has held a series of senior posts within the UK Diplomatic Service. She talks of how she raised her game during her first year as a director. She comments:

I took some risks. If you always felt fully prepared there wouldn't be a risk. I was prepared to learn from others.

I was seeking to make a difference through others. My aim was to get the team to magnify the actions which seemed most important.

Melanie Dawes has held a number of senior positions in UK government departments. She talks of her experience of stepping up into a director general role:

I was asked to step in suddenly and without preparation, and didn't feel like I was ready to be on the Board. I was surprised by how quickly I felt comfortable. My strengths – spotting the strategic questions – worked at the new level and I made some quick wins. The difficult bit was finding the discipline to stop doing certain things. It also took me a while to stretch my ambition and realise how much more I could and should achieve at the new level. I brought in a very experienced HR director who helped me think more strategically. I have learned that my instincts can usually be relied upon – the key is to act on them, not to let things lie, and to embed that as a set of habits. Fully stepping up was a combination of stretching my strengths, getting better at making tough decisions and bringing the right discipline.

For Melanie, the first stage in stepping up was fully recognising her own strengths. She then forged new relationships externally and got other people to help her work out the strategic questions. She was stretching the boundaries by shaping thinking about the issues ever more effectively. She got into the right habits and attitudes of mind and was persistent in asking herself the key questions of:

- To what extent am I stretching to fill this strategic space?
- To what extent am I building people around me who complement my skills?

Melanie wanted to broaden her CV. She had only worked in one organisation and she took the risk of moving to another, leaving the comfort zone of the issues and people she knew. But this stepping out gave her new opportunities on which she was ready to seek to build. What helped were colleagues who supported her and people around her who were as excited as she was about trying to bring a new perspective to solve difficult technical and managerial issues.

Melanie's experience brings together the themes of building on your distinctive contribution, moving out of your comfort zone, taking difficult decisions and building new supporters. She took measured risks; the result was significant, personal growth as well as delivering outcomes in her job that led to promotion.

What happens when you avoid taking risks?

Sometimes not taking a risk is absolutely the right thing to do. When you stand back from the precipice you feel a sense of relief and release as a result of not being foolhardy. But sometimes you can regret not taking a risk. Finlay Scott tells a story of a Territorial Army soldier who was late for training because he had stopped to assist at a road traffic accident and the regular non-commissioned officer sent him home. Finlay regretted he had not intervened because he felt unempowered. The lesson for him was that when you see an injustice being committed, you must be willing to draw attention to the injustice, even if that involves risk.

Can I suggest the following as a useful exercise in assessing your own response to risks:

- What recent risk do you regret not having taken?
- What was the consequence of not taking the risk?
- What held you back from taking the risk?
- What might have enabled you to take a different view in addressing this risk?
- How might you have been better prepared to take a decision about that risk in a different way?
- What was the learning for you as a consequence of not taking the risk?
- What would you do if the same situation arose again in the future?

 Moving forward

- ➢ What have you learned from past risks you have taken?
- ➢ In what ways do you want to be adventurous?
- ➢ What are the benefits of widening your repertoire of approaches and doing things in different ways?
- ➢ How do you best cope with the risk of failure or humiliation?
- ➢ What is the next measured risk you are going to take?

Section C
Up the Pace

Raising your game will involve upping the pace at different points. It will mean building on your preparation and training. It is taking forward all that you have learned so that you:

- *Stretch your muscles*
- *Influence others and convert your critics*
- *Understand how you respond to problems*
- *Warm down thoroughly*

Success when you up the pace requires a subtle combination of your own determination, an ability to influence and persuade those around you, an increased level of self-awareness about how you respond to different problems, and an ability to relax and unwind effectively, whatever the pressures.

At any one time you may feel more confident in one or other of these areas, but if you can take them forward together they provide strength in combination where the overall effect is more than the sum of the parts.

Chapter 9
Stretch Your Muscles

Raising your game requires you to stretch your muscles, although not so far that they will react adversely. Stretching your muscles both strengthens them and enables them to relax more easily. You may need to stretch your muscles in different ways when developing different competences. Doing so can mean chairing a meeting more effectively, building your profile or taking control of a situation. It can mean 'feeling the pain and doing it anyway'.

Why is it important to stretch your muscles?

Muscles that are not used wither away. A muscle that is not stretched becomes useless. Keeping different muscles working well will ensure that your whole body works effectively. Upping the pace necessitates keeping different muscles working in synergy together. At times, some muscles will need to be stretched more than others for the greater good of the whole.

How far have you come?

Sometimes it is important to take stock and reflect on how much you have changed. When June looked back over the last 18 months she said that she was standing on her own more, taking charge and reshaping the agenda more, and becoming increasingly confident in her understanding of how she could make a difference in her organisation. It was as she looked back that she appreciated how much she had been stretching her muscles.

June's growth had not only been in what she had done, it was also in what she had deliberately not done and how in some circumstances she had maintained a tactful silence rather than rushed in with her comments. Part of her new-found strength lay in recognising that what mattered was not what sort of contribution she made, but whether there was a successful outcome. Sometimes that required direct influence from her, at other times it might just require gentle support or steering.

Fiona talked about the effect on her of moving into a new job in raising her game. Stretching her muscles involved taking forward a bigger challenge. She commented:

I knew I could do more. It was important to see clearly what needed to be done. It was seeing the bigger prizes and recognising that to get there you could do some hard things. You cannot make omelettes if you don't break eggs. You have to know how bad it is before you know what needs to be done next. You need to get used to high temperatures. It gives you confidence to deal with a wide range of things.

What does stretching your muscles mean?

Anna Walker has held a number of senior leadership positions, including director general posts in government and chief executive of the Healthcare Commission. Her advice on raising your game is:

Always recognise that you can do things. What makes a difference is being flexible. There is a danger that people go back to approaches that were successful for them in the past, but that may not be what is needed for the next step. You need to learn to do things through other people. You need to recognise quickly what is important and what is not important, what can be left behind, or what you have to do and what your organisation has to do.

You need to be willing to learn from getting things wrong and accept being criticised and learn from it. You need to be able to use different styles and approaches in different circumstances while always having a clear vision for what you have to do. Most people want a clear lead from you.

Practical lessons from the experience of people like Fiona and Anna help you believe that you can rise to the challenge and spot where you can make a difference. They enable you to recognise what is important and learn from it. You need to bring together a clear vision, drive hard towards that vision and continuously gain knowl-edge from what goes well and what goes less well. All this is about holding your nerve, and accepting that you will face criticism but not being defensive about it.

Where might you stretch your muscles?

It can be a valuable exercise to ask yourself every six months or so what the muscles are that you need to stretch. This could mean pushing yourself through a pain barrier in areas, often practical areas, that you have found difficult before.

The rest of this chapter addresses four specific areas where stretching your muscles could be of real, practical value:

- Increasing your chairing skills
- Asking the right questions
- Building your profile
- Taking more control of the situation

Increasing your chairing skills

Have you sat in interminable meetings where the chairperson has completely lost the plot? Have you seen the energy levels in a meeting fall through the floor as the chair wanders off into irrelevance? Enhancing your chairing skills can be done in a number of different ways by:

- Observing good chairpeople and being clear what you are learning from them.
- Experimenting with different approaches and seeing what works well for you.

- Seeking feedback from people you trust.
- Inviting a coach to observe you, talk to participants in your meeting and give you frank feedback.
- Developing your listening and engagement skills.

Box 10 sets out a checklist of questions to ask before, during and after a meeting. The questions cover everything from logistics (room size and table layout), to authority (is there a prompt start and warm welcome?), to the level of energy in room (is the chairperson generating or sapping the energy?). The approach set out in the box suggests doing a self-assessment at the end of a meeting to see how successful it has been, then identify what might be done differently on a future occasion.

Asking the right questions

The most influential people ask the right question in the right way. They articulate the question that goes to the heart of the matter and help someone move on in their thinking and reach a new conclusion. The best question will rarely come completely intuitively. Even a few moments' preparation can lead to a question that hits the nail on the head. Two briefly scribbled questions on a pile of papers for a meeting can be a means of crystallising where you think the focus of discussion and conclusion should be. Often the best questions flow from one another. Once a relationship has been established there can sometimes be a killer question that goes to the heart of an issue and enables the formulation of exactly the right next steps.

Do you create an atmosphere in which hard questions can be asked? Do your team feel that they always have to

Box 10   Meeting Checklist: Questions for the Effective Chair

Before the Meeting

- ❖ Are the logistics right? (basics)
- ❖ Do I have a plan for the meeting? (authority)
- ❖ Who am I going to talk to prior to the meeting? (influence)
- ❖ Am I going to try to manage the different political pressures? (presence)
- ❖ Am I clear about the outcomes I want? (success)
- ❖ How I will create openness and hard thinking? (energy)
- ❖ Am I calm with the courage to crystallise next steps? (impact)

During the Meeting

- ❖ Are the logistics working well? (basics)
- ❖ Am I keeping to time or departing from it for good reason? (authority)
- ❖ Am I steering the course of the discussion appropriately? (influence)
- ❖ Am I responding in the way I want to different pressures? (presence)
- ❖ Am I clear about outcomes? (success)
- ❖ Is there creativity in the room? (energy)
- ❖ Am I clear and courageous? (impact)

After Meeting

- ❖ How do I score myself on a 5 (very good) to 1 (poor) rating on each of the seven steps?
- ❖ What might I do differently next time?

modify the way they put questions so as not to go against the party line or offend? When someone asks you a question, do you hear the intent behind the question?

Box 11 contains a sequence of powerful questions to ask about yourself. Reflecting on the key question in a particular situation for a few moments can be invaluable. It might mean identifying what for you as an individual is the most difficult question to ask.

Box 11 The Power of the Question

❖ What questions do you ask when you have a difficult decision to make?
❖ What are the three most important questions to ask yourself and others before you show your hand?
❖ What are the most important questions to ask yourself:
  ❖ Each week?
  ❖ Each year?
❖ How do you ask a question so that it has maximum impact?
❖ How do you embed in yourself the good practice of asking questions rather than making statements?
❖ How do you embed in your staff the capacity and will to ask good questions?
❖ Are there questions you avoid asking of others and of yourself?
❖ What questions have had the most important influence on you?

Building your profile

Building your reputation is a gradual process, one step at a time. It is based on conspicuous success, but is not just about public victories. Part of building your profile is building trust over an extended period so that people believe your impact is genuine and will be sustained. The following will help:

- Be linked to specific, successful outcomes.
- Be seen to contribute to a range of different projects.
- Be associated with individuals who have been successful.
- Become known for a distinctive type of contribution.
- Develop a reputation for reliability and consistency.
- Develop a reputation for influence within an organisation.
- Demonstrate the ability to hold your own in difficult circumstances.
- Be able to have a consistent impact even when new, unexpected problems crop up.

Taking control of the situation

Taking control is not about dominance or aggressiveness. It is about bringing a measured understanding to difficult situations and being able to influence their direction. It is about contributing clarity and positive optimism alongside realistic expectations. It is about an ability to keep calm and a willingness to be decisive. It is about holding your own while listening to others. Show the following behaviours:

- Be as clear as possible about what the underlying issue is.

- Express clarity of understanding while listening to others.
- Demonstrate that you understand others' concerns while believing that there is a way through.
- Set out a constructive way forward that acknowledges the concerns of others while still being clear in its intent.

 Moving forward

➤ Be clear how far you have travelled.
➤ Learn from others who have taken on larger roles successfully.
➤ Be clear in which areas you want to stretch your muscles further.
➤ Have a clear plan for your next steps.
➤ Keep pushing the boundaries of your competence in developing your skills.

Chapter 10
Influence Others and Convert Your Critics

When you up the pace, influencing others and converting your critics become crucial. You may not think you have much spare time to spend growing your supporters and changing the view of potential critics, but investment in such people can be invaluable. Your default position may be to invest more in supporters than critics, but the views of a sceptic can have a 'bad apple' effect on your reputation. Thinking hard about your approach to sceptics is likely to be well worth the investment. This chapter looks at different ways of building partnerships, growing support from colleagues and improving the relationships with those who are critical of you.

Why is influencing others and converting your critics important?

The more responsibility you have, the more you are dependent on the support of others and the more vulnerable you are to criticism. Investing in and growing your supporters is a crucial part of building and maintaining your reputation. Identifying and either neutralising or converting your critics is central to improving and maintaining your reputation.

This is not about ignoring the preferences of your supporters or the views of your critics. Thoroughly understanding why your critics take the view they do is central to developing your own perspective in a way that is robust and cognisant of other perspectives.

Develop your influencing skills

Who has influenced you most in your working life and why were they able to do that effectively? Often the influence comes through the quality of the relationship, a track record of wise advice, a genuine concern for your well-being and the ability to challenge your thinking in a non-threatening way. Based on your perception of how people have influenced you successfully, how can you develop your influencing skills with supporters and critics?

Key practical steps to enhance your influencing skills include:

- Try to understand where the other person is coming from.
- Give the person your sole, undivided attention.

- Identify what might be the win/win situation for both of you.
- Try to find shared values and base conversations around those shared values.
- Show that you have credibility and insight in areas of particular interest to that individual.

Successful influencing will involve a long game of building respect in others for your experience and creating a trust in shared values. Think about examples of where previous conversations have been productive, and don't expect instant changes in views or behaviours. Judge success by considering outcomes over the long-term and not the short-term.

Be aware of some common risks when trying to influence people, such as being so nice to someone that you lose your focus on the outcomes you are seeking, or becoming frustrated by a lack of immediate success. It's also important to get the timing right. There will be key moments when an individual is ready to change their perspective, and it is not always straightforward judging when that might be.

Sometimes it is a matter of persuading and not just influencing. Some of the requirements for effective persuasion are similar to good influencing, namely key facts and the quality of the relationship. But there is more of a win/lose outcome when persuading, more chance of damaging someone's self-esteem. Key practical steps to growing your skills in persuasion include:

- Structure your arguments clearly and know what your 'killer facts' are.
- Be explicit about the negative consequences if your viewpoint does not prevail.

- Be ready to respond factually and directly to the views of sceptics.
- Build both support for and acquiescence to your ideas with colleagues and stakeholders.

A good persuader will never humiliate those they are working with when they win and will be generous in victory. When they lose an argument, a good persuader will be courteous with those whose views have prevailed to avoid building up resentment. Successful persuasion will involve pacing your interventions, for example, preparing the way to avoid taking someone by surprise and causing them to withdraw or become cross or closed-minded. Listen to the observations of others, sensing when to bring them in as allies. Sometimes members of a discussion or debate 'dig a hole' for themselves or contradict themselves. It's best to allow an individual time to reflect and change their mind in a way that does not humiliate them.

Build new partnerships

Whatever your existing partnerships might be, it is always worth keeping an open mind about building new alliances, particularly during changing circumstances. Sometimes a partnership might be just an informal alliance. On other occasions a partnership might be more of an agreed formal way of two teams or organisations working together so that the joint outcome is more than the sum of the parts.

Key questions to ask yourself as you build new partnerships are:

- What outcomes am I seeking to achieve?
- Who has expertise or a perspective that is complementary to my own?
- What would be the merit of working in partnership with someone else to deliver the desired outcomes?
- What could be the win/win for all those involved?
- How much effort would I need to put into building the partnership, and would it be worth it?
- Would the partnership work best at an informal level or with a more structured framework?
- What is the time period for the partnership?

You need to assess the effectiveness of existing partnerships from time to time, either in open discussion with the other partners or by seeking the views of third parties and those directly affected by the partnership. Using a quantitative measure, however unspecific, can help. For example, asking yourself how you would assess the value and impact of a partnership on a continuum of 1 (poor) to 10 (very good) can focus your mind on how well it is working. Whatever your initial score, asking yourself 'What would need to happen for that score to go up by 2 points?' can be a very useful discipline.

Beatrice, the head of a department in a secondary school, had to work in partnership with other heads of department on various curriculum issues. She assessed the quality of the working relationship with two of her colleagues as 6 out of 10. She concluded that for the score to reach 8 out of 10 she would need to spend more time with these colleagues, looking at shared concerns and reaching a more explicit agreement about how they were going to work together. Her resolve was to meet these individuals for half an hour once every three weeks, agreeing a forward agenda at the first discussion. The result was that the colleagues welcomed the initiative and the quality of the partnership achieved a quick step change.

Building support from colleagues for a decision you want to make

You may have been focusing on a particular issue for some time. You are clear about the preferred way ahead, but you know that you must build support before your suggestion will become the agreed option. Turning general support into specific support on a particular issue involves a positive relationship and addressing the specific issue in the right way:

- Ensure that the ongoing day-to-day relationship with your colleagues is constructive and warm.
- Show continued support for your colleagues in their areas of primary concern.
- Seek their views at a formative stage, listening hard to their perspective and worries.
- Try to reflect some of their issues in your next steps.
- Identify the win/win situation where one of the consequences of getting agreement to your approach is benefits for others.
- Share your proposals at an interim stage, which allows them to be shaped by others.
- Be explicit about the evidence and the value basis for your decision.
- Seek explicit help from colleagues in carrying forward the outcomes of the decision.
- Publicly acknowledge the contribution of your colleagues.

Engaging critics

We all play the avoidance game. We brand someone who criticises us as either ill-informed, irrelevant, outdated, disingenuous, mad, bad or outrageous! In our mind's eye our critics easily grow horns or are doomed to madness or destruction.

A key part of raising your game is to view critics in a new light. The first step is not to be afraid of your critics. Running away rarely helps. Giving yourself time for careful reflection and stabilising yourself is important when the views of critics unnerve you.

Practical steps in handling critics can include:

- Understand where they are coming from.
- Look in a detached way at the relative merits of their perspective and your own.
- Be utterly objective about the strengths and weaknesses of respective positions and potential next steps.
- Be ready to modify your position graciously where the critic is right.
- Take action to reinforce the factual basis of your argument where the critic is wrong.
- Build your supporters and find a context in which to try to work through the issues in a constructive way with your critics.
- Decide on the right balance between engaging your critics, sidelining them and ignoring them.

A possible approach to improving the relationship with someone who is critical of you and demoralises you is set out in Box 12.

It is normally worth distinguishing between those who always seem to be against you whatever the

Box 12   How to Improve Your Relationship with Someone Who Is Critical of You and Demoralises You

Understanding

* ❖ What emotions does this person create in you?
* ❖ Can you separate facts from emotions?
* ❖ What is it like in this person's shoes?
* ❖ What are the pressures on this person that make them behave in the way they do?
* ❖ Is there a pattern in this person's approach to previous situations?

Communication

* ❖ What are this person's preferred means of communication?
* ❖ How do they communicate at their best with others?
* ❖ When do you and they communicate most effectively together?
* ❖ How do you assess the success of different approaches to communication that you have used with them?
* ❖ Would a 'heart-to-heart' discussion help?

Moving on

* ❖ What do you respect about this person?
* ❖ What do you like about this person?
* ❖ Are there situations in which you laugh together?
* ❖ How open is this person to feedback?

❖ Are there any structured changes that could make working together more straightforward?

Learning

❖ What are you learning in this process about yourself, what makes other people tick and different forms of communication?
❖ How would you deal with this situation in an entirely different context?
❖ How would you advise someone in a similar situation?
❖ What more would you like to learn through this experience?

Next Actions

❖ What will be happening if the relationship is working well in six months' time and what will increase the likelihood of success?
❖ Would third-party involvement of a colleague or coach be a help?
❖ What different approaches would you like to try?
❖ What will make you smile as you work with this person?
❖ What are you going to do next this week to build this relationship?

circumstances, and those who support you but are independent enough to give honest feedback. There is a risk of lumping the two categories together. Those who are independent minded are always worth investing in. To deal with those who always seem to be against you, success may be about damage limitation and restricting the impact of their criticisms both on you and your supporters.

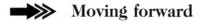 **Moving forward**

➤ Reflect on how you can further develop your influencing and persuading skills.
➤ Consider which partnerships you can grow further.
➤ Think about how you might build support from colleagues for a forthcoming difficult decision.
➤ Reflect on how you have responded to critics and what you would do differently next time.
➤ Consider what practical steps you could to take to improve the relationship with someone whom you know is critical of your approach.

Chapter 11

Understand How You Respond to Problems

As you up the pace you will face new and different problems. These can feel more acute as you may have only limited time to deal with them. You may not be able to do all the research yourself, and will have to become much more reliant on the advice and support of others. How best do you respond to the problems that hit you week by week? You need a high level of self-awareness and strategies that enable you to negotiate well and cope with conflict effectively. Success is about knowing yourself well enough to anticipate how you will respond to problems and how best to prepare yourself.

Why is it important to understand how you respond to problems?

Knowing how you respond in different situations can help you prepare for similar situations in the future. Often your behaviour follows a pattern. Sometimes your reactions might frustrate you, but getting cross about them doesn't help. On occasion you might want to try to modify your responses, but often you just need to learn to live with them effectively.

Clear, practical strategies can help you turn the anguish of a problem into the satisfaction of tackling it well.

Increase your self-awareness

When you face a new problem that you aren't sure how to tackle, it can be hard to admit your uncertainty: it can feel like an admission of failure. However, a consistent message from successful leaders is that being honest with yourself is a considerable leadership strength. Many of us experience the pressure or the sense of obligation to have to 'do it all', but that is reaching for the impossible and can lead to dangerous overstretching. A key consideration is knowing what things you do well and accepting the limits of your capabilities.

As you respond to new and different problems, it is worth reflecting on the following:

• What aspects of your approach worked well?
• What worked less well?
• What might you do differently in the future?
• What might you be less concerned about in the future?

An excellent moment to take stock about your level of self-awareness in addressing problems is when you move from one job to another. Ronald talked graphically about the contrast in how he felt in his new job compared to his old job. In his previous role he had felt under pressure, personally accountable and inward looking. He had addressed problems in a very introspective way and his uncertainty had affected the confidence that other people had in him. His effectiveness had begun to diminish as his confidence spiralled down.

In his new role, Ronald has as a key theme 'I am in control'. He is much more objective in addressing problems. He is more confident and measured in his approach. He sets a more realistic timetable for achieving next steps. He has effectively built a set of supporters who are great sources of encouragement. When he faces criticism he does not take it personally, he addresses it in a straightforward and factual way. He keeps embedding the firm belief that problems are solvable.

Alongside this perspective comes a willingness to acknowledge, to both himself and others, when specific steps are not working and need to be changed. Ronald has a new confidence and a new effectiveness in what he is achieving. He is grateful that people's memories are often shorter than he fears. His reputation has now been rebuilt. Moving to a new role in a new location provided an opportunity to reinvent himself. He is aware of the risks that could lead to a downward spiral again and is determined to protect himself from that possibility.

Keeping an updated picture of how you have responded successfully or less effectively to different problems can help you further refine your self-understanding.

Psychometric assessment can play a useful part in enabling you to understand how you respond to different sorts of problems. The benefits of psychometric tools are

that they can help build self-awareness, highlight preferences and motivations that may not be obvious, and
bring clarity about strengths (enabling you to use the
strengths you have even more). They identify your least
preferred approaches that may need further development
if you are to widen your repertoire of ways of responding
to diverse situations, and they open up issues for conversation about behaviours and responses with which you
might not otherwise be willing to engage.

All psychometric instruments have to be used with
care. One useful personality instrument is FIRO-B, which
measures how you typically behave with other people
and how you prefer them to act towards you. The results
can be used to show patterns of interpersonal behaviour
and expectations and enable you to reflect on how satis-
fied or dissatisfied you are with those patterns. Areas of
interpersonal needs identified by FIRO-B are:

- *Inclusion:* how much you generally include others in
  your life and how much attention and recognition you
  want from others.
- *Control:* how much influence and responsibility you
  want and how much you want others to lead and influence you.
- *Affection:* how close and warm you are with others and
  how close and warm you want others to be with you.

The results cover both expressed and wanted needs. For
example, expressed control is about how often you act in
ways that help you direct or influence situations, while
wanted control is about how much leadership or influence you want others to assume.

FIRO-B provides a snapshot of interpersonal needs that
enables you to be more aware of your natural tendencies

and thereby to choose more deliberately whether a particular behaviour is, or is not, appropriate at a specific time. Reflecting on the conclusions from psychometric assessments like FIRO-B can help you think through how you respond to problems in interpersonal work in groups or on committees.

Recognise how you cope with conflict best

The more you up the pace, the greater the likelihood that you have to deal with conflict. Conflict can be creative and need not be destructive. Out of conflict can often come new options that you hadn't previously thought possible. Preserving your values and self-esteem during conflict is crucial to surviving it.

Key steps in coping with conflict include the following:

In advance

- Be clear about your objectives.
- Be clear about how much flexibility you have.
- Prepare thoroughly.
- Think yourself into the shoes of those with whom you are in conflict.
- Value the support of colleagues.
- Understand your points of vulnerability.

In the moment

- Be clear about your armour and its effectiveness.
- Anticipate the blows and your reactions to them.
- Pace the exchanges and keep up the deep breathing.
- Know how you have responded to conflict in the past.

- Know how you best keep yourself in control in difficult discussions.
- Understand what emotional reactions you are likely to have and how you can keep them under control.

In retrospect

- Embed the learning from what has worked well.
- Recognise the support and encouragement of others.
- Put any conflict into a wider perspective about what really matters in life.
- Allow yourself to take credit for what you have achieved.

A psychometric tool such as the Thomas-Kilmann conflict resolution tool (see www.kilmann.com) can be helpful in assisting you to understand how you respond to conflict. It looks at how you handle conflict using the five strands of avoidance, accommodation, competition, compromise and collaboration. It helps identify how much you naturally need to respond to others' interests and how much value you place on relationships. Some people seem to enjoy being in conflict; the use of this tool highlights that tendency and enables constructive reflection about different approaches to resolving problems.

Negotiate effectively

Developing effective negotiating skills is a core competence for a range of different situations. Effective negotiation is not about beating the opposition into submission, it involves getting a conclusion that is satisfactory for both of you.

Critical steps in effective negotiation are:

- Know the facts well and be clear about objectives.
- Understand what your flexibilities are.
- Build a good working relationship with those with whom you are in negotiation.
- Build up an effective way of negotiating on small issues first.
- Understand why that negotiation process worked and build on what has been successful.
- Agree beforehand how to hold the negotiation (i.e. location, time, numbers of people, pace of proceedings, recognition of outcomes).
- Allow trusted others to observe you as you negotiate and encourage them to give you feedback.
- Be prepared for random events that can throw you off course.
- Mark successful outcomes and learn from them.

Holding firm when courage fails you

There are times when you are dealing with a problem and your supporters seem to drift away. Your courage begins to sag and you wonder if you have been set up to fail. When you have taken a decision and set a course, holding firm when going through a bleak period might be helped by the following:

- Be clear in your own mind why you have made a particular decision.
- Keep your eyes fixed on the ultimate goal, whatever the hesitancy from others.
- Hold on to good things in parallel worlds, so that your life is not completely dominated by this one issue.

- See and enjoy good friends and make sure there is plenty of laughter.
- Remember there are various phases, accepting that some are more torturous than others.
- Imagine there is light at the end of the tunnel and what that would look like.
- Try to stand back and see the situation as objectively as possible.
- Enjoy doing something completely different that might give you energy and will feed back into dealing with this difficult situation.
- Focus on the personal learning and strength that flow from dealing with this type of situation effectively.

➡️≫ Moving forward

- ➢ Keep developing your self-awareness through your own understanding, considering the views of others and occasionally doing some psychometric assessments.
- ➢ Know how you respond to conflict and develop your capability in conflict situations.
- ➢ Reflect on how best to develop your negotiating skills.
- ➢ Recognise how you respond when courage fails you and know how best to handle that situation.
- ➢ Believe that problems make life interesting rather than believing that they will undermine you.

Chapter 12
Warm Down Thoroughly

As you up the pace there will be times of intense activity and concentration. The adrenalin will be flowing as you tackle difficult issues and take complicated decisions. Warming down is crucial so that you do not oscillate from intense activity to complete lethargy. This chapter is about using your energy actively and ensuring that you are able to grow your vitality and have enough reserves for when you need them. It also addresses practical aspects such as managing your time well and coping effectively with stress.

Why is warming down thoroughly important?

For athletes, warming down is about keeping their muscles in good trim. It is pacing themselves so that their body is saved from shocks and has the resilience to handle future intense periods of activity smoothly. You benefit from knowing how best to look after yourself, ensuring good levels of vitality, using time effectively and coping with stress well.

Know how to look after yourself

Often the most successful leaders have very clear strategies for the use of their time and energy when they are not working. They may well bring the same focus to their personal interests that they do to their work. John is a highly effective director general and thoroughly enjoys running a small farm at the weekend. Nick is a confident chief executive who gains enormous pleasure from the work he does on his allotment. Chris is a competent technical draughtsman who particularly looks forward to running half marathons. Anne enjoys her work enormously, but gets even more pleasure from spending time with her teenage children. Ruth revels in her teaching work, but it is the work in her local community and church that provides such an important balance for her.

All of these people are conscious that there needs to be a balance between their work and other areas of life. This might mean using some of the same competencies in both worlds or it could mean bringing a very different set of skills and preferences. They might need to be a leader in the working world but a supporter and encourager in the world outside work. They might make a supportive contribution in their working world and take a leading role in community or family activities.

Julie Taylor has had a sequence of very demanding director roles. When asked what her advice is on how to raise your game, she said, 'Learn to relax.' For her, knowing how to look after yourself involves these behaviours:

Get in touch with a state of mind that allows you to be the best version of yourself. Learn to manage your own emotional state. Build up habits and disciplines that keep you in equilibrium and enable you to relax. Get the feedback loop right so that things don't get out of proportion. Remember that anxiety is nobody's friend.

Grow your vitality

What are the sources of energy in your different spheres of life? They might be your family, your community, your faith, physical recreation, wider intellectual interests, the arts and music or hobbies such as photography. In many of these spheres there may be something that enthuses you. Part of the test is whether something engages your full attention and whether you feel better or worse for spending time on that particular activity. There will be difficult choices between relative priorities, particularly when the wider family is involved. The key issue is what activities outside family and work responsibilities are most precious in recharging your batteries, giving you an equitable perspective on life, providing humour and lightness, and enabling you to do your work even better because you are that much more fulfilled.

Growing your vitality is about identifying what activities have the most beneficial impact on you, and then seeing if it is possible to do more of those activities in a way that benefits both you and those who are most important to you.

How can you best ensure that you use your energy levels in the most effective way at work? It might be of value to assess yourself against questions like:

- When in the day are you at your most productive?
- What sort of rhythm of work best energises you?
- How important is variety within your working day?
- What is the best use of gaps during your working day? Is there an opportunity for a quick five-minute walk?
- Do you use your lunch break to recharge your batteries?
- What do you do if your energy begins to flag?
- Do you receive advance warning if you are beginning to be tired? Are you aware of how this affects your judgement?

It can be helpful to reflect on the relationship between your vitality and time spent in your comfort zone. Sometimes spending time in your comfort zone is a source of energy and renewal, but equally important is stretching your boundaries. The athlete who runs a half marathon in 90 minutes may well be energised by the prospect of running it in 85 minutes on the next occasion. For others, running a half marathon in 90 minutes is achievement enough and provides a sense of well-being and vitality without needing to strive for even higher standards of achievement.

In a booklet entitled *Thriving in a Faster, Faster World* (Praesta, 2007), Heather Dawson talks of leaders building in time for their 'oxygen tent' or 'oxygen pocket', which could be a hobby, a physical endeavour, a cultural interest or a charitable work. She talks of the oxygen tent as a form of 'enlightened self-interest', providing a space for renewal in the 'hectic business of leading organisations'.

What are the oxygen masks that keep you in equilibrium? When you are busy at work it might be a brief walk at lunchtime, a photograph of a mountain or your children on your desk, an exchange of smiles with a good colleague, a brief telephone call with your spouse or partner, or reflecting briefly on a job well done. Using your oxygen mask is a necessary part of survival, but if you use it too often you become overdependent on it. Knowing it is there and available is a great reassurance.

Knowing what your oxygen mask is and using it is a sign of strength, not weakness. It is worth considering:

- What is your oxygen mask?
- When has it been useful?
- How regularly do you use it?
- How can you ensure that you do not become too dependent on it?

Manage your time effectively

Jennifer was very conscious that her life was demanding, with pressure to go from one meeting to another. She decided to commit herself to a number of practical steps, which included:

- Putting two clocks on the wall in her office so that everyone in a meeting could see them.
- Trying to arrange meetings to be 50 minutes or 20 minutes in length, giving her 10-minute gaps between meetings.

- Ensuring that participants knew of the time constraints in advance so that they could prepare to use the time well.
- Having breathing moments between meetings, which might involve walking a little more slowly from one meeting to another.
- Preparing more in advance so that she was clearer about what she wanted out of meetings.
- Reflecting on what moments gave her particular joy and how to recreate them.
- Being as clear as possible in her own mind about what she could fix and what she was not going to be able to fix, and therefore ensuring that she focused on the possible.
- Distinguishing clearly between when she had responsibility for particular actions, and when she had delegated that responsibility to others.

The consequence was more focused interventions, better use of time and more energy. Those brief moments of 'warm-down' during the day became very precious as her life got even busier.

At the heart of effective time management is forward planning, prioritising, focusing, delegating, influencing and being tough. Practical steps on each of these are summarised in Box 13.

Coping effectively with stress

Pressure can be a very positive driver. Stress can be an unwanted and unhelpful response to pressure. You may sometimes feel that stress is an unavoidable reaction in a difficult situation and you may recognise pressure for

Box 13   Practical Steps to Manage Yourself and Your Workload

These are the key questions to ask when looking at the effective use of time and energy.

Forward Planning

- ❖ What are the outcomes or goals that you need to deliver over the next year?
- ❖ How is success defined as far as your boss is concerned?
- ❖ Where are the biggest gaps between what is expected of you and where you are now?

Prioritising

- ❖ Where can you add most value? And which are the things that only you can do?
- ❖ Where can you unblock things for the benefit of others?
- ❖ What are the most difficult challenges you need to tackle?
- ❖ How can you prioritise so that your energy is devoted to sorting out these difficult tasks?
- ❖ Are you honest enough to know when you are stuck on an issue and you need help to sort it out?

Focus

- ❖ Can you enhance your ability to bring concentrated focus to one issue to solve it in a systematic way and then move on to the next issue?

❖ Can you develop the ability to switch from one thing to another and remain totally focused and absorbed in each successive task?

❖ Can you train yourself to give your sole, undivided attention so that a short time with an individual means quality time?

Delegate

❖ How much more can you delegate?

❖ How will you ensure quality of outcomes in what you delegate?

❖ How do you ensure that delegation is not abdication of responsibility?

Be Tough

❖ Are you sometimes too willing to take on responsibilities from others?

❖ Could you be tougher, saying no to peripheral requests?

❖ Could you be tougher on yourself to avoid getting involved in tasks that others can take forward perfectly well?

what it is in a range of different situations. However, you do have a choice about how you react. This is not only about what you do physically but also how you think mentally and feel emotionally.

Arnie Skelton, in 'Eliminating Stress' (*Public Service Magazine*, 2008), recommends exercising regularly, talking your concerns through with supportive others, knowing how to relax and switch off, learning to let go of anxiety and worry, putting fun into your life regularly and discovering 'absorption techniques' for deflecting your thinking from negative to positive by having something else to think about. He sets out some practical suggestions, including:

- Remove yourself from provocations that you find difficult to manage.
- Check your views on people and life, including yourself: are you looking for downsides or upsides?
- Be careful about the language you use in discussing stress: avoid saying 'I've got a stressful job' because it becomes a self-fulfilling prophecy. Choose to say 'pressure' instead of 'stress' in order to emphasise that pressure is inevitable, but stress is not.
- Choose, learn and then practise calming techniques, so that when faced with a provocation that tends to 'get you going' (e.g. a difficult colleague), you have internal resources that you can call on. For example, breathe more deeply and slowly, and engage in positive self-talk ('I can do this' rather than 'I just wish the floor would open up ...').

➡️➤➤ Moving forward

- ➤ Know your own pressure points.
- ➤ Recognise your sources of vitality and increase them.
- ➤ Develop a pattern that uses and renews your energy well at work.
- ➤ Recognise signs of stress and be willing to take action against them.
- ➤ Never regard a break or relaxation as a waste of time.

Section D
Grow the Momentum

This section is about growing your momentum. You have upped the pace and now it is important to grow the momentum even more. Some of the most important elements are:

- *Keep your focus*
- *Grow your resilience*
- *Build your team*
- *Renew your freshness*

You are in this for the long haul. You have made good progress, but there is a long way to go. These elements are crucial so that you are seen to go from strength to strength and reach the goals you have set out to achieve.

Chapter 13
Keep Your Focus

We are forever getting diverted by interesting or irritating things. We are addicted to email, our Blackberry or our mobile phone and as a consequence are always flitting from one thing to another. The immediate is forever driving out the important. How do you cope with this relentless pressure so that you keep your focus on what is most important? This chapter looks at the sort of focus you are looking for to ensure successful action, take hard decisions and build in effective communication.

Why is keeping your focus important?

Being clear about your focus will increase your likelihood of success. At the same time, you need to guard against focus leading to being blinkered and ignoring key new information or perspectives. A rigid focus that takes no account of changing circumstances can be just as dangerous as no focus at all. Focus may need to be tempered by flexibility. You may need to review how new information and changes in circumstances affect your focus and the outcomes you are trying to achieve.

What sort of focus are you looking for?

Giles was very clear what contribution he wanted from the chief executive. For him, the role of chief executive involved setting direction and vision, resolving difficult issues, steering the business, sorting out systematic issues, ensuring effective networking and partnerships both internally and externally, building a strong reputation for the business, and ensuring effective upward management of the chairperson and the board.

All of Giles' prerequisites were about the chief executive focusing effectively; he did not want a chief executive who was vague and unclear about their priorities. Giles wanted to be working for a strong leader with a clear sense of direction, but he was also conscious that a focused approach should not be inflexible. As economic and political events were likely to occur at speed, he wanted a leader who was listening carefully and was willing to adapt their approach, while being rooted in core values and clarity about the overall objectives that the business had set itself.

Claire had inherited a leadership role in an organisation where people were unenthusiastic about change. External pressures meant that change was inevitable. What was the best way of getting people on board? Should she bring a strong focus on new outcomes or would it be better to listen longer to what people had to say? Claire was conscious that she needed to ensure that people were motivated and willing to go with her. Therefore, her initial focus was going to be on recognising the need for change rather than laying down a precise prospectus at this initial stage.

Claire set out her approach, which included the following:

The world is changing, we need to be at the centre of that change. We need to be clear about the big picture and develop our direction of travel. We need to work together to get ourselves into a position where we drive change. We need to develop an even more open and collaborative way of working with other parts of the organisation and with our customers. We need to build on our success but be realistic about the inevitability of change. Change will happen whether we like it or not: we need to be leading it, and be at the forefront of change. We need to be practical in the way we ensure that we deliver the results we want. There is a role that needs filling: we must not leave a void, we must believe we have a positive contribution to make.

These examples emphasise the importance of a focus that is realistic, believable, inspirational and yet rooted in effective listening to those affected. It is important that you are able to take people with you and avoid the risk of walking the gangplank with everyone else waving you goodbye.

Ensure effective action

Allan Leighton wrote an excellent book entitled *On Leadership* (R H Business Books, 2007), which draws on his experience as a leader and on interviews with many chief executives. He summarises the leadership lessons from individual leaders in a few, short bullet points for each person. Many of them share a common theme of ensuring effective focus. Key leadership lessons from Philip Green (Arcadia and Bhs) are absolute focus, learn from people, don't complicate things, have the respect and trust of staff and be reliable. For James Dyson (Dyson International) the leadership lessons are never give up, make it very clear what you are doing and why you are doing it both publicly and internally, and recognise that sometimes you cannot make a big leap but only lots of little improvements that in the end add up to a big improvement.

Charles Dunstone (Carphone Warehouse) talks of creating a team that gels and a vision that everyone can believe in and ensuring a common sense of purpose throughout the organisation. For Stuart Rose (Marks & Spencer) the leadership lessons include look for heroes, doers and people who can take the ball and run with it, never be seduced by your own success or believe your own publicity, and keep your antennae switched on 24 hours a day in and out of the business.

For many successful leaders in every sector, there is an unremitting focus on outcomes and delivery. When you are clear what can make the biggest difference to success, a relentless focus on the key levers will lead to the best possible likelihood of achieving that success.

Take hard decisions

Tough decisions come in many different shapes and sizes. Any leader or manager has to make decisions about strategic direction, resourcing, communications and the management of staff. Taking hard decisions well requires a high level of focus on what you want to achieve and how you are going to get there.

It is possible to develop your capacity to make hard decisions. Here are ten key steps to help you focus on this difficult area:

- Observe others making decisions and note down what they did that worked well and what worked less well.
- Be objective and base decisions on firm evidence, even when that evidence is contrary to what you had previously assumed.
- Understand your convictions and apply your values, intuition and trained judgement. Recognise that facts have a wider context of values and beliefs.
- Build up self-knowledge, understand your own strengths and weaknesses, but don't get caught up in a spiral of self-analysis.
- Learn from experience. Whatever decisions you take, note three or four learning points from each, whether a decision has gone well or badly.
- Be willing to take decisions. Don't be caught up in indecision, going through the same arguments again and again.
- Grow your courage, step out into the unknown and see opportunities.
- Develop your communication skills and your listening, engaging and persuading skills, without falling into the trap of appearing to manipulate people.
- Build sounding boards using a range of different people who have different perspectives and skills.
- Obtain quality feedback given in a positive and supportive way. This can be one of the most valuable gifts you can receive.

When you have made a difficult decision it can be well worth asking yourself the following questions afterwards:

- Did I focus on the right pieces of actual input?
- Did I focus on the perspectives of the right people?
- Was the balance between focus and flexibility right in the way I made the decision?
- Have I focused enough on the likely consequences?

Ensuring an effective focus for communication

Good communication starts with listening. Building understanding, networks and partnerships involves continuous listening and engagement. Don't just focus on the eventual outcome, the final point of announcement. Success depends so much on a sequence of steps and effective focus and communication are needed at each stage.

The following questions might help you focus on the importance of communication in any decision:

- Am I listening effectively to all the sources of intelligence available to me?
- Am I building partnerships and alliances with the right mix of people?
- Can I develop my approaches in building partnerships and consensus?
- Can I strengthen my ability to engage effectively with a wide range of different people? Am I learning how best to communicate outcomes from decisions I see being taken?
- Can I further develop my sources of feedback?

 **Moving forward**

➤ Know what outcomes are most important to you.
➤ Be conscious what helps you keep a focus on the right priorities.
➤ Always be clear about the key points of action that come next.
➤ Be clear how you want to develop your capacity to take hard decisions more effectively.
➤ Keep refining your ability to focus on what matters most when you take hard decisions and communicate outcomes.

Chapter 14
Grow Your Resilience

Resilience is about coping with the buffeting that comes from decision making in a faster world. It involves holding firm to principles and values when all around seem to be losing theirs. It is about not letting the gremlins get you when you are struck by self-doubt or fear part way through a task. Growing your resilience involves recognising that you are in it for the long haul, pacing the use of your energy, knowing how to recover from defeat and being conscious what your self-worth is based on, so that criticism becomes positive input and not destructively negative.

Why is growing your resilience so important?

Long-distance runners develop their stamina through regular training and building up a high level of resistance to pain or exhaustion. Resilience is a combination of resistance to pain and recognising the benefits of what you are trying to deliver.

Build resilience

Gordon McDonald has held a number of different leadership roles in government organisations. His resilience has grown through successive demanding jobs. He comments:

> It is important to take opportunities. It is spotting them when they are there. It is taking a deep breath and then a leap. The trick is not to overanalyse every situation: you sometimes have to jump.
>
> It is important to trust your own instincts. When someone mentioned a job to me I felt excited about it. It instinctively felt OK. I had a positive, gut feeling. It is important to remember that nothing stays the same. If you are doing a job that is comfortable you do have to remember that you will have to move on. It is important to move on to the right job at the right time. Sometimes, even if the time is not quite right, it can be important still to move on. You want to avoid the thought: 'What if I had been bold enough to go for something, what would that have been like?'

Resilience is the most under-rated aspect of leadership. It is important you stick with it. When the going gets tough you need to keep telling yourself it will be OK over time.

Resilience allows leaders not only to accept change but to learn and thrive in it during great challenging times. It enables them to demonstrate flexibility, durability and have an attitude of realistic optimism. Resilience means dealing effectively with challenging circumstances, seeing uncertainty as an opportunity and not a threat.

How resilient are you? Ask yourself:

- Am I pacing myself and taking care of myself physically? Challenging times can be protracted, so eating and sleeping well is crucial.
- Instead of ten trips of one day, is it possible to do four or five trips of two days each, allowing better-quality time for people and less wear and tear on me? This may seem easier said than done, but avoiding unnecessary 'virility tests' can be very important.
- Am I looking after my self-esteem? Those with mental strength will be giving lots of support to others and thereby ensuring collective survival, not just their own.
- Am I recognising what gives me vitality outside the work situation and allowing that source of vitality to grow, whether it is around family, community, faith, sport or recreational interests?
- Am I protecting enough time for me as an individual to breathe, reflect, be encouraged and uplifted?
- Am I recognising the positive anchors in my life and nurturing them unashamedly?

Developing your own resilience can include looking out to see how others are coping. It can mean encouraging others to find their own ways of looking after themselves and building resilience when under sustained pressure. This can have a mirroring effect, raising your own level of resilience.

Recover from mistakes

Any individual who has never made a wrong decision is either arrogant, blind to the impact of their actions or lying! Although your life may be littered with wrong decisions, in one sense there is no such thing as a wrong decision if you ensure that you gain effective learning from all the decisions you make.

When you have made a mistake, remember:

- Admit that you have made a mistake and do not try to cover it up.
- Stop digging holes for yourself by making the situation worse.
- Be clear what your learning has been through this experience and demonstrate through your words and actions what you have learned.
- Be conscious of the audit trail. Be explicit as to why you made a particular decision and the considerations you were taking into account.
- Be ready to position yourself differently on the next decision of a similar nature so that you do not fall into the same trap again.
- Ask others how they have moved on after they have taken wrong decisions.
- Allow yourself to be encouraged by the experience of others.
- Accept that some people will blame you.
- Accept that you may be able to move on more easily than others.
- Try to draw a line under the event in your mind so that it does not become a recurring nightmare.

Regard every experience of a decision that goes wrong as an invaluable part of your life.

Building resilience for the future

In his book *On Leadership*, Allan Leighton records a key leadership lesson from Mark Thompson, the chief executive of the BBC: 'It is not the hit but your reaction and recovery time that will make a difference.'

This point is a very telling one. If you take a knock, others will notice it. How you respond will reflect on how your contribution and leadership are perceived and will also influence the way others behave. If your colleagues and staff see you as resilient, they are likely to mirror the same behaviour. If they see you disappearing defeated, that will be their inclination too. This is not about macho behaviour that ignores current reality or suppresses your honest reaction, but about engaging with your vulnerabilities in private rather than in public, at least in the first instance.

Acknowledging how you have responded to knocks and moved on can be a very powerful message. The impact is often greater as a completed story told after the event rather than sharing anguish widely as it happens.

It is worth reflecting on the following questions:

- How strong is your current level of resilience?
- What has developed your resilience recently?
- What are the greatest risks of your resilience being undermined?

■➤➤ Moving forward

➤ Be clear how you deal with your vulnerabilities.
➤ Know what types of conversations, reflections or reading enhance your resilience.
➤ Know the people whose presence can best strengthen your resolve.
➤ Be self-aware of the effect that mistakes have on you and how you recover from them best.
➤ Be explicit about the practical steps you might take to build your resilience.

Chapter 15
Build Your Team

As you build your momentum you will be build-ing your own team. Some of the team members will be reporting directly to you, while others may have a more informal link. In order to get the best out of your team you need to be clear about what value-added contributions you are looking for. Sometimes you may need to keep your team renewed and nurtured. Building your team suc-cessfully involves a combination of decisiveness, delegation and serving the team.

Why is focusing on building your team important?

If you try to operate in isolation you will drown, over-whelmed by work and exhausted through lack of encour-agement from others. Raising your game successfully means putting significant time into the hard work of team building. Recognise that this is always a dynamic process, with team membership changing and evolving. A team that is too stable can easily become stagnant; the challenge of new ideas and new blood is essential in any team.

Getting the best out of your staff

When focusing on getting the best out of your staff, ask yourself 'What can I do for them?' rather than 'What can they do for me?' Henry, a senior leader in a law firm, talked about trying a range of techniques to motivate someone to work more effectively when she looked as if she had no desire to raise her game. Eventually she did make a step change, but it was because she wanted to change, not because her boss wanted her to change. Henry learned that you have to enable people to arrive at their own motivation based on their own interests and goals. Then they are much more likely to step up to the responsibility and be willing to drive positive action.

During challenging times, a key question is how individuals' strengths and networks are to be used effectively. Who is going to lead the operational aspects? Who is going to be doing the negotiation with stakeholders? Who will be responsible for communications? Define roles, maximise energy, benefit from people's capabilities and avoid the debilitating effect of organisational muddle. Flexibility will still be important, but within a framework where everyone knows what they are expected to deliver.

Ideally, within any team you should make time and space to identify individuals' motivations and build the pattern of work around their preferences. Sometimes a more direct approach is necessary when time is short and a range of different tasks need to be done. Where there has been scope for individuals to identify their own preferences in the normal course of work, they are more likely to be willing to do particular tasks when the situation requires decisive action. Clarity about a leader's reasons for a more direct approach will be important; this may not need to be explained at the precise moment when urgent action is required, but an explanation later can make a big difference in terms of an individual's feelings.

In challenging times certain people within a team come to the fore; it helps if you know who they are ahead of time. It may well be those who have been through similar situations in the past and have 'worn the tee shirt'. How are they going to be deployed? During busy periods you might need to adjust your expectations about people in your team. The stress will incapacitate some but take others to new levels of competence.

Toughness when leading a team is crucial. Be relentless in delivering outcomes, be willing to prioritise and then prioritise again. Listen to people's concerns, demonstrate a good level of understanding and be willing to adapt where possible in response to the suggestions and concerns of team members.

When the going gets tough in any team there can be a danger of being soft on underperformance. If someone is not coping with a demanding situation it is no help just leaving them in a bad place. Sometimes painful conversations with team members are necessary both for the organisation and individual. Someone may need to be moved out of the team, but this should only be done for reasons that you've carefully thought through and explained.

You can feel sorry for people who are struggling and tend to avoid the emotional pressure of difficult conversations, but sometimes tough conversations are essential.

In his book *The Five Dysfunctions of a Team* (Jossey-Bass, 2002), Patrick Lencioni talks of the five themes of:

- Absence of trust
- Fear of conflict
- Lack of commitment
- Avoidance of accountability
- Inattention to results

These five strands have proved crucial in many different team situations. Key questions to consider as you build a team are:

- How can trust be built more strongly across the team?
- How can you ensure that different views can be expressed openly and honestly, which allows difficult issues to be explored constructively?
- How can the level of commitment of individuals be grown more strongly (or a limited level of commitment identified and action taken)?
- How do you ensure clear lines of accountability that are visible and accepted, with agreed methods of updating them over time?
- How do you ensure that results are clearly measured and transparent and lead to effective feedback?

Practical steps for addressing each of these five themes are illustrated in Box 14.

Box 14   Enhancing Team Effectiveness

Build Trust

❖ Individuals develop mutual understanding of each other's preferred and less preferred ways of working.
❖ Individuals work on shared projects together and are honest about what has worked well or less well.
❖ There is a strong emphasis on explicit praise when action goes well and honest feedback when mistakes are made.
❖ There are good informal as well as formal links between individuals.

Legitimising Conflict

❖ Robust discussion is encouraged on discrete issues.
❖ Role play is used as a means of bringing out different ways of viewing particular problems.
❖ Individuals are asked to talk explicitly about what types of conflict they are at home with and when conflict can affect their judgement detrimentally.
❖ There is honest reflection after robust debates about how the process worked.

Build Commitment

❖ There is clarity about the shared vision.
❖ Opportunities exist for people to talk about what they are particularly committed to.

❖ Individuals are encouraged to articulate what is motivating them in different situations.
❖ The level of commitment that people put in is acknowledged as well as the outcomes.

Ensure Clear Accountability

❖ Accountability arrangements are explicit from the outset.
❖ Team members say to what extent they are comfortable with their accountabilities and how they are going to fulfil them.
❖ External feedback provides a check on whether accountabilities are being fulfilled (no health check is ever wasted).
❖ Accountabilities are modified in the light of changed circumstances, but it is always done transparently and never fudged.

Focus on Results

❖ Robust figures are provided for results.
❖ Results are visible so that they speak for themselves.
❖ Individuals have full opportunity to talk through why their results are as they are.
❖ There is always opportunity to define new steps to deliver the required results.

Bringing a healing touch

Many teams need a 'healing touch'. There can be under-lying prejudices, resentments, fears, frustrations and even anger that get in the way. Because of past history or future apprehensions, there is possibly reluctance among some team members to get close to other colleagues. These inhibitors mean that some teams never operate at their full effectiveness because of a sense of underlying reserve or even suspicion.

How do you help bring healing to your team?

- Enable individuals to understand each other better and work more effectively together.
- Assist people in understanding why they have preju-dices or perspectives that they bring to particular situ-ations and decisions.
- Enable the team to leave past failures behind and move positively into the future.
- Create defining moments when a team moves from a 'half empty' perspective to a 'half full' affirmation.
- Enable people to address their fears and apprehensions openly.
- Use the trust you have with individuals to encourage them to change their attitude towards people who may have hurt them or forgive those who have let them down.
- Encourage those whose confidence has been dented to forgive themselves and move on.

Being a 'good doctor' is not necessarily bringing about a magic solution. Instead, contribute practical wisdom, encouraging your 'patient' to heal themselves through their actions and attitudes. The 'leader as healer' may sometimes have solutions they want to offer, but often the most useful medicine is a reflective and honest conversation that helps an individual move on from past frustration and anger. While the healing role of a leader can be hidden, (its effectiveness only partial visible because it is done quietly), it can still have a very powerful effect.

➡️≫ Moving forward

➢ Build 'buy-in' to the outcomes sought.

➢ Build trust between team members.

➢ Encourage honesty and open debate.

➢ Allow team roles to evolve due to external circumstances and individual contributions and be explicit about how roles are evolving.

➢ Always regard team membership as evolving and accept change as inevitable and right.

Chapter 16
Renew Your Freshness

Growing your momentum will involve intense, prolonged activity. The danger is that a resolute focus on delivering particular objectives can lead to you being blinkered and bored. Running the eighteenth mile of the marathon is hard work and drudgery with the destination far out of sight. What keeps runners going is having their eyes fixed on the goal. But where does the freshness come from to lift their spirits and maintain their resolve? Freshness is about staying open-minded, knowing when to forget, coping with disappointment and keeping up vitality.

Why is renewing your freshness important?

As you raise your game, guarding against staleness and boredom is vital. If your heart sinks your mood can spiral down into your boots. When your motivation wanes, every step becomes even harder work. Knowing what keeps you fresh means that you are alert and able to accept change and knocks in a positive way.

Staying open-minded

Hazel Mackenzie is a well-respected facilitator who helps leaders reflect on how to keep up their motivation. Her advice is practical:

> *Beware of putting a label on yourself. You are in danger of boxing yourself in. If you describe yourself as being disorganised you will be disorganised. You never look as bad or as good as you think; reality is in the middle. Recognise that your mood swings might be flights of fancy rather than reality. Watch the spiral. When you are fluid and confident you will become ever more effective.*
>
> *Observe yourself. Be mindful of what is happening but don't believe you have to be perfect. Watch the avoidance tactic and beware when it distorts your approach. Be conscious of the difference between want and need. I want something is much more motivating than I need to achieve something. Always be conscious about what is giving you energy.*

Hazel's constant theme is about keeping up freshness and allowing there to be a spiral upwards, leading to hope and a positive approach, rather than a spiral downwards, leading to dejection and the likelihood of failure.

Being fresh is partly about being confident in your own ideas. It is a step on from merely relying on picking up ideas from others. Freshness is about being open to new ideas and approaches, recognising that there is often more than one way of solving a problem. It involves recognising what gives you energy and how you can nurture those sources of energy, and acknowledging what thought processes enable you to view problems in different ways. Accept that you will feel a different level of freshness depending on the time of day and your location.

The authors of *?What If! How to Start a Creative Revolution at Work* (Capstone, 1999) set out some practical examples to help you develop fresh ideas:

- Take a new form of transport to work next week. You will be amazed who you can meet and what you will see.
- Deliberately read a magazine or newspaper, listen to a radio station or watch a TV programme that you wouldn't normally see. Children's TV is good for this.
- Plan a monthly lunch with people from other parts of the business whom you don't usually consult. Chat to them about an issue they are working on and get their perspectives on issues you are working on.
- Get out of your normal environment for at least half a day a week. At least 70% of what we think is the result of what is around us.
- Ask your family (especially kids) to help solve a problem you are working on.
- Allocate twice as much time as you normally would to solving a problem. Make sure that you have three solutions before choosing one.
- Block out 'freshness time' for you and your team once a month. Go somewhere you wouldn't normally go together or do an activity you wouldn't normally do.
- Take a walk in the park during office hours. Change the pace of your thinking. Take time to ponder.

- Listen to pop charts. Do you know what is No. 1 at the moment?
- Reinvent your role at least twice a year.

Some of these ideas will not appeal to you. You may be more interested in classical music rather than listening to the pop charts, but the question of what stimulates you to fresh thinking is a good one.

Enhancing the skill of forgetting

How good are you at forgetting? Forgetfulness can be dangerous when you have made commitments to others and you have obligations to meet, but it can be a strength when it allows you freedom to invade your mind.

The ability to forget is crucial to moving on. If you remembered every number plate you had ever read, your mind would be completely cluttered. You have to forget facts to allow room for new facts to be remembered! But you also have to forget some of your emotional reactions. So often your mind can be cluttered with emotions like anger, resentment or frustration about past events. You might feel that you have been unfairly treated by your organisation (resentment), that you have not been able to achieve what you wanted (frustration), that you have been bullied by a particular leader (anger) or that you might fail on a particular project (fear) or you may not be able to get a past failure out of your mind (pain).

Emotional clutter in your mind can be a very damaging inhibitor. You can get stuck and be unable to move on. Your emotions can become so fixed or frazzled that your scope for freshness has completely gone.

Progress comes through recognising what your emotional reactions are and reflecting on how you can best leave them behind. It happens when you are honest about what anger, resentment or frustration is gnawing away at you. You can then box that emotion, talk it through with a good friend or coach and decide on the best way for you to move on. You need to recognise that the past is the past, decluttering your mind from irrelevant facts or destructive emotions and then giving yourself space to have a genuine openness to new experiences.

Coping with disappointment

As your responsibilities grow you will experience a mixture of successes and failures. You will strive towards certain outcomes and feel dejected and disappointed if they are not delivered. Part of moving on from disappointment is recognising that the process of being disappointed allows you to be honest about your emotional reaction when something does go wrong.

Key steps in coping with disappointment can be:

- Be conscious of your normal pattern of how long disappointment lasts.
- Try to define the sources of disappointment as tightly as possible.
- Be conscious about what in the past has helped you move on from disappointment.
- Always think about the silver lining to this cloud.
- Be explicit about the practical steps you need to take to move on from the disappointment.

- Hold fast to the original reasons for taking a particular course of action and decide whether you want to give it another go.

Keep nurturing your successors

It is not only renewing your own freshness that matters, it is developing freshness in others. A nurturing parent is clear on the boundaries, but always caring in their app-roach. Nurturing is about growing other people so that they are strong and decisive, with attitudes and decisions rooted in a transparent set of clear values.

Nurturing will involve strong messages but will also include care, compassion and positive support.

How can you increase your capacity to nurture others and keep them fresh?

- Be willing to share your experience of what works and what doesn't work.
- Be open about revealing how you handle your own vulnerabilities, fears or priorities.
- Set aside time to mentor others in focused conversations.
- Bring together groups of people who can learn from each other.
- Become an even better listener and be prepared to ask different kinds of questions that enable people to develop their own confidence and competence.
- Reframe what you regard as success so that it includes the outcomes achieved by those you have nurtured.

The leader who nurtures others will build up a genuine and substantial bank of support and goodwill.

Enabling others to keep fresh will in its turn have a valuable impact on you. The more you legitimise others keeping open to new ideas, the more they will want to share them with you and stimulate you to develop your own clarity of expression.

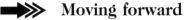 Moving forward

- ➤ Think about whether you are being too rigid in your thinking.
- ➤ Reflect on what new ideas you have been open to at the end of each week.
- ➤ Decide who stimulates fresh thinking in you and ensure that you have regular conversations with them.
- ➤ Recognise what facts or emotions are cluttering your mind and holding you back from fresh thinking. How can you further develop the skill of forgetting?
- ➤ Nurture others to bring freshness to their own thinking.

Section E
Where Next?

In this section we move from growing the momentum into making decisions on where to go next. There are times when it is right to take stock and reflect on your journey so far and think about what you want to do with your life next.

This section considers four key themes:

- *Keep an open mind*
- *Recognise when the tide turns*
- *Know what matters to you*
- *Renew your vision*

When you feel there is a loss of momentum or impetus in what you are doing it can be more difficult to reflect and stand back, but there is a danger that when the momentum is strong it may take you straight into a brick wall. Keeping an open mind and recognising when the tide turns can be particularly important. Knowing what matters to you most will give you a frame of reference when decisions need to be taken and will enable you to make choices well. Renewing your vision needs to be an ongoing evaluation if you are to retain your energy and vitality.

Chapter 17
Keep an Open Mind

Maintaining a strong focus on the outcomes you want to deliver will mean that you have a greater chance of success. Focusing your drive and energy on what you think is right will help give you a strong sense of fulfilment. But keeping an open mind can also be a powerful corrective. It involves knowing when to step back, being honest about your options, recognising what the break-points are and being ready to be surprised.

Why is keeping an open mind important?

The pace of change is such that the right focus one year may become outdated by the next. Keeping an open mind is about being aware of changes in the external world, changes in your own economic and emotional well-being, changes in the perspectives of friends and family, and developments in your own preferences. Keeping an open mind does not mean keeping an empty mind.

Allowing yourself to reflect on new ideas or approaches will enable you to keep an open mind. Accept that there will always be scope for developing the way you think and act.

Know when to step back

Prianga had a track record of success in her job as a college lecturer. She was very single-minded and got excellent results from her students by driving them hard and expecting them to respond to her demanding approach in a thorough and responsible way. Her students had always done well and Prianga was very proud of her own accomplishments.

But her students' results began to stagnate and then fall back. Her demanding style was not as popular as in the past and she did not find it as easy to motivate her students. Prianga felt that her professional pride was being hit. The immediate effect was that she became even more relentless in the classroom and began to get more pushback than in the past. A good friend encouraged her to step back and reflect on what was happening to her students.

Prianga put her personal pride on one side and began to be more conscious of the effect that she had on her students. She very deliberately decided to alter her style, injecting some humour and more overt compassion. She allowed a greater degree of warmth to be shown in her teaching while keeping the same tight structure in her approach. The result was that her students' results began to go up again. Prianga was glad that the friend had advised her to step back and reflect on the approach she was taking. She was relieved that she had been open-minded enough to make adaptations to her approach that had the desired effect.

How good are you at stepping back?

For some people, the best activity to help them stand back is quiet reflection, for others physical exercise and for others one-to-one dialogue or conversation in a group. What matters is that you decide what works best for you:

- Are you best at stepping back alone or with someone else?
- Who helps you stand back most effectively: is it a mentor, a coach, a family member, a close friend, a colleague?
- What physically do you need to be doing to stand back: resting, sitting, walking, running?
- How open are you when you stand back and how willing to modify your preferred approach?
- What is your track record of being willing to stand back and change direction?

Be honest about your options

Being honest about your options is never easy. Some people fall into the trap of being perpetual dreamers, never spending long enough on an idea for it to crystallise and for the pathway to that outcome to become clear. For others, the risk is the opposite: they can be so focused on the day to day that the option to do something markedly different never catches their imagination or seems like a realistic option.

Keeping an open mind is about dreaming dreams. Let your imagination take you to new roles or new places, allow yourself to build on success and take opportunities when they arise. Be bold enough to keep climbing the mountain because you believe that there will be a fantastic view when you get to the top. Nevertheless, for those dreams to have relevance it is important to maintain a sense of reality, not to squash a dream but to 'give it legs'. What are the practical next steps necessary to help increase your prospect of success?

Being honest about the options is about raising your sights. Allow yourself to believe that there could be something good to follow on from what you are currently doing. Believe that you have talents, experience and expertise that others are going to value. Know that what you bring to the party is worthwhile, even if it may not be immediately recognised by yourself or others.

Are you honest about the options? Asking yourself the following questions can help:

- If I have a tendency to dream dreams, how can I keep up the stimulus of new ideas and yet root them in what is realistic?
- If I don't dream enough dreams, how can I allow myself to dream a dream or two?
- What three or four options do I have about next steps in my job?
- If I do not think I have any options, what would I like the options to be?
- What do good friends think are the options?
- What options would it be good to explore a little more?
- What timetable would I like to set myself to be clearer about potential options?

• What would being one step more radical than my natural inclination actually involve?

What are the breakpoints?

You can be in danger of thinking that whatever your current situation is, it will go on forever. But time moves on remorselessly and no team stays the same for very long. There are going to be comings and goings and financial situations will go up or down. People's moods will change. There may be a growing demand for what you do or demand may drop off in an unpredictable way.

It is often useful to take a hard-headed look at potential future breakpoints. A range of breakpoints could include the following: What might a new financial year mean for your business? What are the critical points when customer demand will mean that you have to make radical changes? What would be the effect of key people retiring or moving on? What will specific anniversaries mean for you in terms of length of time in a role or age? At what point are there likely to be significant changes in your domestic situation and what effect will they have: your spouse seeking to change their job or a youngster going off to university?

You may find it worthwhile reflecting on:

• What are the breakpoints in your external world that are likely to affect you the most?
• What are the breakpoints that matter to you in terms of your role, responsibilities and age and at which you want to take stock?
• Do you want to set breakpoints for the future when you will re-evaluate your priorities?

- How best do you respond to breakpoints and how do you want to prepare for them?

Be ready to be surprised

When I moved from being a director general in government into executive coaching, I had a clear plan. What took me completely by surprise was the opportunity to write books and articles. When I work as an executive coach with individuals at points of transition, I encourage my clients to develop a plan based on their strengths and the opportunities they see ahead, but I also encourage them to be ready to be surprised. New opportunities may present themselves, someone else might recognise a particular skill in them that they could use in new ways, and changes in the external world can mean that new, unexpected possibilities appear.

   You might find the following a very practical set of questions to ask yourself:

- Am I open to surprises?
- What have been some of the best surprises I have had?
- What has surprised me about what friends and colleagues have noticed I'm particularly good at?
- How willing am I for surprises to take me off into new ways of thinking, believing or acting?

➡≫ Moving forward

- ➤ What is the best way for you to stand back?
- ➤ How honest are you about your future options?
- ➤ What are the breakpoints that are coming up for you?
- ➤ How ready are you to be surprised?
- ➤ How open-minded are you willing to be?

Chapter 18
Recognise When the Tide Turns

You may be clear where you want your destination to be. You might think that you have a very clear pathway ahead of you, but then all of a sudden the direction doesn't appear quite so straightforward. The distant horizon has been replaced by the swirling fog in front of you. It now feels as if you are looking through a glass darkly. What was once certain has now become uncertain. The fixed points have begun to disappear, your champions are nowhere to be seen. It is not always that easy to get used to the fact that the tide has turned. Sometimes it is only by forcing yourself to be patient that you are able to recognise that a tide can ebb and flow.

Why is it important to recognise when the tide turns?

Living with the ebbs and flows of life is inevitable. When life is going your way, be thankful for your good fortune and take opportunities when they arise. When life doesn't go your way, keep your equilibrium and don't allow your well-being to be destroyed. Taking knocks will not be easy, but accepting the inevitability of the ebbs and flows of life can build your enjoyment of what is good and your resilience to cope with what is painful.

The strong swimmer will develop the capacity to go with the flow, stand up to the waves, avoid drowning, come up for air or move to a different bay. These capabilities also apply to an individual reflecting on where to go next.

Go with the flow

Going with the flow means that the swimmer reaches their destination more quickly than their arms alone will carry them. It means having a clear line of sight and modifying your trajectory to take account of the prevailing current. It involves recognising that sometimes you are in the right place at the right time and able to take full advantage of the situation to take you forward to the next place.

When you have champions, align yourself with them and follow in their slipstream. Success from going with the flow is not about complacency but about investing in networks, colleagues and supporters so that you build up a bank of goodwill for the future. Going with the flow is about being optimistic and seeing change as an opportunity and not a threat. It might mean making your own luck by having the confidence to see opportunities where the water flows strongly in one direction.

It also means bringing generosity of spirit to situations and people, and not trumpeting your own good fortune. What is important is to keep your champions, be at the right place at the right time, follow the opportunities and invest in your supporters.

Stand up to the waves

Swimming against the tide is no fun and requires dogged endurance. Standing up to the waves is part of coping with happenstance. You may be facing wave after wave of problems or criticism that appears relentless. Part of coping with it comes from believing that the storm will not be for ever. It is accepting that there may be a succession of pounding waves with repeated blows to the chest and that you may have to 'roll with the punches' for a while, drawing on your stores of resilience. Believe that the storm will pass and hold on to your self-belief.

Avoid drowning

An experienced swimmer will keep a rhythm in their breathing and avoid taking unnecessary risks. Try not to get out of your depth and ensure that you have trusted friends along with you who will spot the signals if you begin to get out of control. Hold onto your values and the rhythms of life that keep you going. Don't panic even when the waves grow stronger and threaten to engulf you.

Success is about holding on to your strengths and using them in a focused way. Be ready to cope with random events, be supported by trusted friends, and seek coaching so that you are kept sharp and efficient.

Recognise the ebbs and flows

A good swimmer will also know about the ebbs and flows of the tide and will take account of the currents as they plan their swim. Success as a leader is often about recognising those ebbs and flows. Sometimes you are in the wrong place at the wrong time: success then is recognising that reality and moving on. You can be hugely successful one year and be regarded as a failure the next. You are the same person bringing the same attributes, but fashions or moods alter and reputations can change rapidly for little apparent reason.

Recognising the ebbs and flows is about accepting that life is not fair. You may have striven hard to reach one objective, but as you get close to that goal the wind has changed and you find yourself going in the wrong direction. Moving on involves accepting that you may need to make a fresh start.

Believe that even when the tide is against you, it will turn; that cycles can be broken and that all of a sudden there can be a breakthrough. It might be helpful to see failure as the start of the tide turning and accept that there can be new life when that happens.

Come up for air

How strong are your lungs? An experienced swimmer needs to come up for air on a regular basis. Sometimes you may think that success in dealing with a situation is all about keeping your head down and using your energy to keep on a predetermined trajectory, but breathing fresh air is crucial. You need to be taking in new sources of energy and developing that lung power.

Coming up for air is about persistence and continually seeking a necessary intake of oxygen. Draw inspiration from 'parallel worlds' so that energy in one area can permeate other areas of your life.

Move to a different bay

Even the strongest swimmer may decide that the time has come to move to a different bay. The pounding of the waves and the strength of the tides may be a source of exhilaration or exhaustion. Switching to a new place can be a recognition of reality and not a sign of weakness.

When external events have begun to erode your energy or credibility, it may be right to say 'enough is enough'. If relationships are broken, it might not be worth the investment to repair them. Sometimes you need to accept the reality that the tide has turned. Is it time to reinvent yourself, to seek new sources of energy or to deploy your strengths in a new way in a new place, while remaining true to the values that are most important to you?

Be ready to move on. Allow yourself some curiosity about what swimming in new waters will be like and believe in your ability to cope with any major change that will bring.

You will recover again when the current begins to flow in your direction.

Is the tide turning a good thing or a bad thing?

Sometimes when the tide turns it can create new beginnings, at other times it can feel like previous hopes are being dashed. Abdul had had a sequence of very interesting jobs. He had built a network of supporters who always spoke well of him. He seemed to be on a pathway to great success. He had just been appointed to a very big role, but then his boss left and the replacement wanted to bring in his own team. So for the first time Abdul tasted rejection and removal from a post to which he thought he was well suited. His first reaction was one of anger followed by depression. There was a danger that his crossness and his dejection could have got out of hand. Because he had never been rejected before, the emotions were high in their intensity.

Abdul gradually came to terms with the situation, helped by wise counsel from different friends and colleagues, and he now regards this incident as one of the most formative of his career. It made him realise that success was not guaranteed and that it was not only what he managed to deliver that mattered. He recognised that he could be at the mercy of other people's decisions and preferences, which was a hard lesson to take. Abdul became a more resilient and stronger individual as a result of this experience. He recognised that living with the tough times was just as important as taking advantage of the good times.

When the tide is going your way, find time to ask yourself some key questions:

- How do I maximise 'going with the flow'?
- How best do I keep my humility when things are going well?

- How do I take advantage of the good times and build up my capabilities and resources for the less good times?
- How best do I support those who are struggling when things are going well for me?
- How best do I guard against self-satisfaction and keep up my generosity of spirit?

And when the tide turns against you:

- How can I hold my nerve in these situations?
- How best do I guard against any feeling of resentment or anger?
- How best do I keep my sense of perspective and allow life to be influenced by my values rather than my vanity?

The person who can keep their equilibrium through good and bad times is the person best equipped to deal with whatever life throws at them. Observing yourself to see how you have coped when the tide turns on small things (like success or failure in a particular task) can help you prepare for when the tide turns on big things (such as losing your job or major changes in your family situation).

➡️ ≫ Moving forward

➤ Accept that tides ebb and flow.
➤ Remember how you coped when the tide turned before.
➤ Recognise what values and relationships are most important to you when the tide turns.
➤ Accept that good can result when the tide turns.
➤ Keep your sense of humour anyway.

Chapter 19
Know What Matters to You

You can keep going on a fixed track without properly evaluating what really matters most to you. You may not properly examine questions like: Where does ambition fit into my life? How important is recognition or achievement? Where do family and friends fit in? How important is financial security to me? People rarely stand back and consider the freedom of choice they have. You may have more freedom to choose than you allow yourself to believe. Reviewing what matters most to you is an essential part of deciding where to go next.

Why is it important to know what matters most to you?

When you are focused on a particular task or job you can become blinkered. Sometimes thinking through what is important to you helps you clarify and simplify situations. You have to be honest with yourself about your motives; there has to be congruence between what you say matters to you and your decisions and related behaviours. You can so readily deceive yourself if you are not careful.

Where does ambition fit in?

Ambition is not a negative thing. Society needs motivated individuals who are ambitious to be head teachers, medical consultants, scientists, judges and mechanical engineers. Without ambitious people our economic and political systems would collapse. But if ambition means that individuals become too single-minded or are ignorant about the impact of their actions on others, it can lead to a sense of failure and dejection.

Healthy ambition means working hard and being focused. But also consider the effect of your ambition on others as well as its impact on your own health and well-being. Ambition that is unfulfilled can become a source of unhappiness or the starting point for the next phase of your life.

Talking about ambition can be uncomfortable. Start by asking yourself these questions:

• What is the focus of my ambition?
• Why am I ambitious in this way?
• What would be the effect on me if the ambition were unfulfilled?
• What other ways are there of fulfilling my current ambition?
• What is the perspective of family and friends on whether my current focus is a sustainable ambition?

There are times when an ambition needs to be reframed. A top scientist may move from wanting the accolade of personal discovery to leading a team effectively and then to mentoring young scientists. A lawyer's first ambition may be to be a good barrister, then to be a good judge and later a presiding judge, looking after the well-being of other judges. How open are you to letting your ambition evolve over time, perhaps moving from individual achievement to enabling others to deliver outcomes effectively?

How important is recognition?

We all need recognition, although we don't always admit our dependency on it. We can be deeply offended if our presence is not acknowledged or we are not invited into a discussion.

Bob was very conscious that his level of confidence suffered if his contribution was not recognised. While he never wanted to blow his own trumpet, he became dejected if he was ignored. He was aware of the issue and was probably more on top of it than he admitted. He knew intellectually that he could rely on his positive reputation and did not need to seek recognition every week, but it was less easy to realise this emotionally. Gradually he accepted that recognition was not going to be about glowing words of praise but was about others noticing what he said. He taught himself that recognition was about gradual influence and not about seeing dramatic changes directly attributed to his interventions.

Sometimes it is important to redefine the type of recognition that is most important to you. Elements of recognition might include a brief nod when you make a good point, a gradual shift in your boss's view of you, a quiet word of thanks from one of your clients or customers, or a smile from someone who has accepted your wisdom. Make sure that you are alert to the sources of recognition around you, and take heart from them when they appear.

Where does financial security fit in?

Whatever people earn, they tend to compare themselves with those who are paid more. They always see their salary as less than it should be. Somehow the system is unfair and they are not getting their just reward. How easy it is to fall into this trap of only comparing yourself with those who are better off than you. Financial security is important. You want to provide for your family, you have come to accept certain luxuries and you see holidays as an investment in your wellbeing. Travel is your right as part of living in the twenty-first century.

But what are your real financial needs? What is a necessary level of income for the lifestyle you want to live? How much is left over to invest for the future? Where does charitable giving fit in? Does your personal conviction lead you to give away part of your financial assets for the well-being of others?

Honesty about your aspirations is important in the way you use your financial resources. If there are fixed points about where you live, where your children are educated, what healthcare provision you want to provide, these need to be reflected in your goals and ambitions. On the other hand, raising your game may mean lowering your sights in terms of financial assets: what matters to you may be more time with family and friends or working a four-day week so that you can put time and energy into voluntary activities. Ask yourself:

- What level of financial security is important to me?
- How much of my financial income am I willing to give away for the benefit of others?
- What would be the effect of deliberately living at a lower level of financial expenditure?
- How do I balance financial well-being with other aspects of well-being that are important to me?

Embracing the freedom to choose

Your ability to choose varies at different stages of your life. In your 20s you are free to make all sorts of choices about jobs, friendships and partners. In your 30s and 40s you may find yourself living with the consequences of those decisions. In your 50s the opportunity to choose resurfaces as your pattern of work changes or children leave home. Often these changes will not be of your own choosing.

Your choices may be more limited than you would like them to be, but you always have the freedom to choose your attitude. You can decide whether the conclusion of one job is the beginning of the end, or the start of a new opportunity. The freedom to choose your attitude is a precious gift. Think about what choices are available to you and to what extent you want to make choices about your future.

Carole was doing a worthwhile job for a charity. Her contribution was often commented on, as she was always thorough and reliable if not that adventurous. Sometimes she felt that she was being taken for granted. There appeared to be no opportunity for advancement within the charity, as it was small and people rarely moved on.

Encouraged by friends, Carole began to reflect more closely on her skills and decided that it was time to look elsewhere. She started hesitantly and then more confidently. When she realised that she had a choice about whether to stay or go, it ironically had the effect of making her more assertive within the charity. The charity began to view her in a different way and offered her an enhanced role!

 Moving forward

> ➣ What is your current level of ambition and how do you want it to change?
> ➣ To what extent are you captive to the need for recognition?
> ➣ To what extent is financial security an issue you want to address?
> ➣ How much do you want to use your freedom of choice?
> ➣ Is choosing your attitude to success or failure an important next step?

Chapter 20
Renew Your Vision

However clear the vision you have this year, you are likely to need a renewed vision next year. Alterations in the external world because of economic changes, globalisation, the speed of transfer of information and shifts in political expectations come faster and faster. Your values give you fixed points, but your vision will need to be continually developing as expectations of you change and your ability to contribute evolves over time. If you do not renew your vision you stagnate. Refreshing your vision and reinventing yourself can give you new energy.

Why is renewing your vision important?

A battery needs to be recharged or it will go flat. Your energy levels need to be recharged if you are to sustain your energy. You need to be re-inspired so that you can focus on the outcomes that are most important to you.

An opportunity to take stock can enable you to achieve a new perspective on what it means to be successful.

Observing others renewing their vision

My first career was 32 years in the UK Civil Service. When I had the opportunity to move into a second career as an executive coach at age 55, it represented a renewed vision and others saw in me new energy and vitality. Taking this step into a new career was a life-changing moment and involved a completely new vision of myself making a difference through coaching senior leaders.

It is encouraging to see individuals develop a new vision or expression of themselves. Andy moved from teaching into adult tutoring, Peter moved from banking into teaching, Julia moved from being a solicitor into teaching, and Margot moved from being a doctor's surgery receptionist into church ministry.

As you observe individuals transferring from one sphere into another, you can sense their renewed vision and energy. Watch it, it can be infectious!

When is reinventing yourself important?

Reinventing yourself is not about taking on a completely different personality. Each of us has something unique about our character. Your essential 'Charlieness' or 'Sarahness' is central to your personality and success. Reinventing yourself is not about changing the essential you, but it could mean adapting your approach significantly to fit different contexts.

Now may be a moment to make a radical change in your approach. For example, you may have received feedback that you could become a better listener. When entering a new job you might decide to listen more and use practical techniques to ensure that this happens. You might want to invite feedback after a few months to see whether people now regard you as a good listener or not.

Reinventing yourself is also about using the opportunity of a change of job or role to step up. You may be conscious that you are not as confident as you would like in your job: you are feeling your way and learning about the organisation. But in your next role you can build on the experience that you have and be a more surefooted and assertive leader.

What about when you start a new job?

Starting a new job can be an excellent moment to reflect on what you want your impact to be and how you want to present yourself. In advance of starting a new role, ask yourself these key questions:

- How will success be defined by my new boss?
- What are the outcomes I want to deliver after six months?
- What might be some early wins?
- What are the most important relationships and how do I want to build them?
- How can I make a good first impression, and how do I want to be viewed after three months?
- How will I keep up my energy and freshness and ensure that I have a realistic work/life balance?

I often ask individuals when they start a new job what adjectives they would like people to use to describe them.

I then ask what evidence they will have that will mean that these adjectives have been applied to them. Addressing these issues allows you to decide how you want to live your values in the new role. What is then important is to get feedback a couple of months into the job and find out whether those you are working with use these adjectives to describe you!

Renewing your vision partway through a role

You may not have the opportunity to reinvent yourself by switching roles. You might be expecting to teach in the same village school for a number of years to come; you might be the vicar in a parish expected to stay another four or five years; or you might be building up your practice as a solicitor and have no intention of moving to a different location. What does reinventing your vision mean in these circumstances?

- What are the changed expectations of you and your organisation?
- What different aspects of your work energise you most now and how can you build on those?
- What are the next tasks on which you would particularly like to focus?
- What will give you greatest joy in your work in the future?

Reflecting on these questions can help you take stock and decide what type of renewed vision you want to focus on. Often you need a stimulus to generate a new vision, which could include a sabbatical in a very different environment, a quiet retreat in a monastery or on a mountain top, periods of silence when you allow what is most important to you to dominate your thoughts, or structured conversations with a coach that help you decide on your next steps.

Enabling others to renew their vision

Even if you originally decide there is no need to look at your vision, it might be that as you enable others to think about their own next steps and renew their vision, you are stimulated to do the same. As you give you receive. As you see others excited by new possibilities and with a new focus and energy, you can catch something of their new life. It can be infectious if you play a part in enabling others to renew their vision!

The impetus to renew your vision can come through external stimulus or inner change. It often arrives through the external stimulus of a change of role, a new boss or different expectations, but is can also arise through inner change stimulated by reaching a certain age, the death of a close friend, as a consequence of honest comments by friends, family or colleagues, or as a result of a profound religious, emotional or intellectual experience.

Responding to inner change is not a sign of weakness: it is a recognition that your beliefs and priorities will change over time. Being open to inner change is a sign of maturity as you remove the blinkers of past attitudes and allow yourself to be open to new directions.

➡≫ Moving forward

- ➢ What are you learning from others renewing their personal vision?
- ➢ How important is reinventing yourself?
- ➢ What scope is there within your job to renew your vision from time to time?
- ➢ How might you enable others to renew their vision?
- ➢ How will you know when you are running on empty?

Section F
To What End?

What's it all about? What is the purpose of all your activity? It's a long time since you took your first steps: you've been upping the pace and growing the momentum ever since. At various times you have thought about what next, but really – what is it all for?

The themes of this section are:

- *What is fulfilment for you?*
- *How do you want to be remembered?*
- *What about family and friends?*
- *Where does joy fit in?*

As you read through each chapter, do allow yourself time to reflect on the purposes of the activities you are engaged in. Why are you bothering: what are the deep-seated drivers or values within you that keep you striving towards making a difference? Do those who are special to you get enough of your time and energy? Is there as much joy in your life as you would like? If not, what can you do about it?

Chapter 21
What Is Fulfilment for You?

What is a fulfilled life? Where does success fit in? Is success part of fulfilment or a distortion of it? When you seek fulfilment are you looking for false horizons and not living enough in the present? How can you enjoy the present to the full as well as being on a journey on which you are seeking to make a difference? Where does hope fit in: is it just a denial of the importance of living in the present? What aspects of fulfilment are most important to you? These are some of the questions that inevitably strike people from time to time. Often you may dismiss them as you focus on day-to-day business, but if they go unanswered you can be left with a heavy heart, regretting that you did not take the time to think them through.

Why is it important to be clear on what fulfilment means for you?

Understanding what fulfilment means for you gives you a framework for deciding the most important way of spending your time and energy. A key consideration is the balance between the short-term and the long-term. You can be very fulfilled by the tasks of a particular day, be it the lecture you are giving, the patients you are seeing or the projects you are overseeing. But having a clear understanding of what might be your fulfilment in the longer term can help you shape the short-term and provide you with a sense of perspective and purpose.

Recognising what you are driven by

When asked in an interview if she had any 'personal drivers', one candidate replied that she did not have the luxury of a chauffeur! But maybe some of your personal drivers are like chauffeurs who take you to destinations where you may, or may not, want to go. The drivers for success or recognition can be strong positives when giving you a focus for your energies, but they can also be negative if they distort your behaviour and destroy your perspective.

George felt a strong drive to become a college principal and he focused his time and energy around that. He was at the cutting edge of curriculum development and built networks both locally and nationally. He was willing to support his colleagues because he thought that was the right thing to do, and because it had the side benefit of enhancing his reputation. At one stage

George was working excessive hours on a long-term basis, giving himself virtually no respite at the weekends. He began to ask himself why he was driven so much. Health problems gave him a shock and made him stand back.

George did not modify his ambition of wanting to become a college principal, but he was able to set his ambition into a wider context. He took up regular physical exercise, renewed friendships outside the professional educational world and stopped doing some of the less important networking. The result was that his ambition became better focused; he was a more cheerful and healthier individual with a wider range of interests. He did become a college principal, but was immensely grateful for the 'wake-up call' that allowed him to re-evaluate his priorities and put his sense of drive into a wider context.

I like the comparison in Box 15 between the calming words of Psalm 23 and the hectic words of 'Not Psalm 23', which may bring you up short as you reflect on how driven you sometimes are!

What does making a difference mean?

When you have family responsibilities, a prime purpose of work is raising funds to live on and provide for your family. A happy, well-fed and cared-for family is a perfectly legitimate kind of fulfilment. But can fulfilment be more than that? Fulfilment can be a job well done; delivering outcomes you had not thought possible; influencing the direction of the team of which you are part; and enabling others to do their job well. It might be worth reflecting on:

Box 15   Recognising What We Are Driven By

Psalm 23

The Lord is my shepherd, I lack nothing.
He makes me lie down in green pastures
he leads me beside quiet waters,
he refreshes my soul.
He guides me along the right paths
for his name's sake.
Even though I walk through the darkest valley.
I will fear no evil,
for you are with me;
your rod and your staff,
they comfort me.
You prepare a table before me in the presence of my enemies.
You anoint my head with oil;
my cup overflows.
Surely your goodness and love will follow me
all the days of my life,
and I will dwell in the house of the LORD
for ever.

'Not Psalm 23'

The clock is my dictator, I shall not rest,
It maketh me lie down only when exhausted.
It leads me to deep depression,
it hounds my soul.
It leads me in circles of frenzy
for activity's sake.
Even though I run frantically from task to task,
I will never get it all done.
For my 'ideal' is with me.
Deadlines and my need for approval,
they drive me.
They demand performance from me,
beyond the limits of my schedule.
They anoint my head with migraines,
my in-tray overfloweth.
Surely fatigue and time pressure shall follow me
all the days, hours and minutes of my life.
And I will dwell in the bonds of frustration
for ever.

Written by Marcia H Hornok

- Where do you believe you have made the biggest difference over the last year?
- Over the next year where do you think you could have the biggest impact?
- In what areas of your life will making a difference give you the greatest satisfaction (e.g. in your work, with your family, within your community or through your personal interests)?

What is your life purpose?

For some people 'What is your life purpose?' is a helpful question, for others it is a turn-off. For some, the notion that they have a life purpose determined other than by their own action is superstition, for others they believe that there can be a life calling that it is right to seek after.

Jayne felt that she had a life purpose to be a doctor, which gave her a very specific aspiration. Her grandfather had been a doctor and was a good role model. Other influences on her were her school, her parents, her enjoyment of biology and a fascination with medical ethical issues. This collection of factors reinforced the belief that her life purpose was to be a doctor. She followed her dream, which helped motivate her when the studying became more difficult.

Isa had felt a strong sense of life purpose to become a barrister and was utterly single-minded in approaching this goal, but she found it very difficult to get a pupilage in chambers and, when she did, she struggled to get enough clients. Eventually she accepted that she had to change direction, as the courtroom was not the place where she excelled. Isa reframed her expectations and became a very fulfilled solicitor. She recognised that while her sense of life purpose had helped get her through a law degree, she had to adopt a revised sense of it to take account of practical reality.

Where does faith or belief fit in?

For some people this is a central question, for others it is irrelevant. Faith is not about leaving your judgement behind, it involves working through issues about what life is all about. For many people faith in a loving God provides the context and meaning for their approach to life and work. When individuals dismiss faith as irrelevant, then they can be missing a whole dimension of fulfilment.

Questions to ask yourself might be:

• Does the faith dimension have a place in the way I seek to contribute and see my own fulfilment?
• Do I understand how the faith dimension influences the approaches of those I am working with?
• Is there more I would like to do to develop my understanding of the faith dimension as it affects me personally or those I am working with?

 Moving forward

➢ What are you being driven by and how is that changing?
➢ What is the biggest difference you would like people to describe you as having delivered?
➢ Does a sense of life purpose have any resonance for you?
➢ Are there aspects of the faith dimension you might explore further?
➢ How do you measure your level of fulfilment?

Chapter 22
How Do You Want to Be Remembered?

One day you are fully immersed in solving a problem. Time moves on and two weeks later that problem has been overlain by many others. A year later the problem that was all embracing is long gone and your contribution has been forgotten. How do you want to be remembered? What is the legacy that you want to leave in your job? How can you best move on and leave others to take the action forward?

Why is it important to reflect on how you want to be remembered?

Part of the context for this question is recognising that you will not be remembered for long. Your contribution will be rapidly superseded, although there are times when you can make a difference that will have long-lasting implications. A teenager will remember for the rest of her life the youth worker who helped her embark on a different direction. A patient will remember the surgeon who helped save his life. A company will long remember the creative contribution of the inventor who changed its direction.

What do you want to be remembered for?

When a group of staff were reflecting on a chief executive who had retired 10 years earlier, they were not talking about the individual decisions he made or how he handled specific issues, what they were discussing was his enthusiasm and passion. They talked about his words of encouragement and the long-term impact of some of his feedback. What they were remembering were the emotions of their relationship with the former chief executive and the impact he had on them in terms of their own careers and their learning.

It is now five years since I completed my time working as a director general within government. When I come across individuals who used to work in the directorates for which I was responsible, they sometimes tell me stories about how I influenced them. Often I cannot recollect the instance, but it is a continual reminder that it is the way we interrelate with people that will be remembered well after the particular reason for the exchange.

It can be worthwhile asking yourself these questions:

- How are those I meet likely to remember my contribution over the last year?
- Is that the way I want to be remembered?

- How does this perspective change the way I want to interact with people over the next year?

These questions are not about encouraging you to be soft on people, they are inviting you to think inside the shoes of other people in order to understand what contribution is likely to have the biggest impact on them. Those who remember you most are likely to be those whom you have encouraged and stretched in their thinking.

What is your legacy as you move on from a particular job?

How you leave a job can have long-term effects. When you have been appointed to a new role, your preference can be to move as rapidly as possible into the new job. Some, like government ministers, shift instantly into a new role and have no time to complete unfinished business. Normally you have a period when you know that a transition is about to happen and you have the opportunity to complete tasks in progress.

When Darren was told that he would be starting a new job in four weeks' time, his immediate inclination was to think about all the tasks he personally needed to deliver. His immediate emotion was dejection, as he knew that it would be impossible to complete them all. His focus then switched to how best he could transfer to others the responsibility for delivering the next steps so that his role became enabling rather than delivering.

What 'added value' could Darren really bring over the next four weeks? He decided to spend one-to-one time with the people working for him in mentoring conversations, enabling them to work through their own next steps and giving them clear feedback. These perspectives were not contaminated by his expectations as a boss. Because he knew he was going to another post, it released him to give personal development time to all his staff. A final reflection from Darren was that perhaps he should have committed this quality time to his staff sooner!

When you move on to a different role it might worth reflecting on:

- What is the legacy you want to leave behind?
- What are the loose ends you should either tidy up or pass on before you go?
- What are the specific tasks you need to finish off?
- How can you best mentor key individuals before you depart?

The final words of farewell are so important. A good blessing at the end of a religious service sends people out in a positive frame of mind. The final 'benediction' you give when you leave a job will influence the way people view subsequent tasks and will also affect how they view you over the long term. Just as a good funeral for someone who has lived a full life is a reflective and joyful occasion, so marking your departure with a sense of celebration as you move to a new job enables both you and your colleagues to move on positively to the next phase.

Getting it all into perspective

However much passion and energy you put into a job, at the end of the day it is only a job. You can so easily end up with an inflated view of your own importance and the value of the work you do. Yes, you are making a difference, things are better because of your contribution, but in the great scheme of things yours is a modest drop in a large ocean.

Getting a job into perspective is not about diminishing its importance, it is about being realistic and recognising that your contribution is modest and purposeful.

And while your contribution may have been a drop in the ocean, that drop might have quenched someone's thirst and given them new vitality.

 Moving forward

➢ Ten years after you have left your current place of work, how do you want the people you worked with to remember you?

➢ When you move on from your current role, how do you want to be remembered?

➢ If you were to leave your job in a month, how would that influence your current use of time?

➢ Is there more you might do to mentor people?

➢ What does 'getting it all into perspective' mean for you?

Chapter 23
What About Family and Friends?

In the hard-nosed world of business, politics, colleges or hospitals, it seems a distraction to talk about personal relationships with family and friends who are most important to you. Where do relationships fit in when you are having a demanding time at work? Love is about how you treat those around you, be it in your family, your community or at work. It is also about loving yourself in a way that nurtures and does not abuse.

Why is it important to focus on family and friends?

You may think that your family and friends will always be there, so is there a danger that you take them for granted? Nurturing relationships with family and friends is rarely a wasted investment in the long term. Strong bonds of love and affection with those who are important to you will keep you grounded and able to put the pressures of the day into a more measured perspective.

Where does love fit in?

Love is not about inconsequential gossip, it is about respect for other individuals and supporting them through thick and thin. Love comes from mutual regard, shared values, emotional empathy and a shared sense of being on a journey. In the words of the first letter to the Corinthians:

> *Love is patient, love is kind. It does not envy, it does not boast, it is not proud. It does not dishonour others. It is not self-seeking, it is not easily angered, it keeps no record of wrongs. Love does not delight in evil but rejoices with the truth. It always protects, always trusts, always perseveres. (1 Corinthians, Chapter 13, verses 4–7, NIV)*

Love is about how you order your life and bring discipline to the way you look after yourself and those for whom you care. Love is having practical compassion when that is needed and not judging people when they are down. As well as bringing encouragement, love might involve challenging people to think in new ways within bonds of companionship, and not out of competitiveness or spite.

A popular song a few decades ago spoke about love 'making the world go round'. Empathy, companionship, mutual support and looking after each other provide the means through which you rub along in harmony and not in discord with colleagues. Without a combination of respect and affection, organisations soon slip into discordant relationships. At a personal level, without love you are a fractured and muted human being.

So cherish those closest to you. Give up aspects of your ambition when your family and friends need you and order your priorities so that you have quality time with the young people in your life who are important to you. The flexibility provided by IT today gives a much greater opportunity to be flexible in your working patterns and to be with family members at times most important to them.

Some key questions might be:

- When are your family and friends more important than your work?
- When do you give your best quality time to the young people in your life?
- How readily do you listen to family and friends about what is most important to them?

Do you love yourself enough?

Loving yourself sounds indulgent, but it is about respecting yourself and being concerned about your physical, emotional, intellectual and spiritual well-being. If you love yourself, you enable your body, mind, heart and spirit to be refreshed and renewed. Practical things to think about include:

- Can you use weekends more to build the bonds of love with your family and friends and to relax?
- What are the activities that will provide renewal and relaxation and be special times with family and friends?

- What types of reading, travel or music will relax you and mean that you are more open to the companionship of others?
- What type of place enables you to be at peace with yourself and be renewed?

 **Moving forward**

➤ Who are the people whose well-being matters most to you?
➤ What would you give up for any of those people?
➤ What habits or disciplines might you develop further that would reinforce bonds of love with those most important to you?
➤ How does the importance you attach to family and friends influence the way you use your time?

Chapter 24
Where Does Joy Fit In?

Joy is not just about sudden bursts of hilarity. Joy is a deep-seated sense of being at peace with yourself, the experience of being with others at a level that is cheerful, purposeful and engaging. Joy makes you feel uplifted and able to cause a sense of buzz in others. It is about recognising what makes you laugh and using your smile to make others smile. Your own joy is enhanced as you create a sense of joy in a team.

Why is it important to know what gives you joy?

Joy takes you out of yourself and enables you to believe that difficulties that seem impossible and demanding will be a worthwhile challenge. An inner sense of joy reinforces your resilience and enables you to show courage you had never thought possible. Without joy, life would be a terrible drudge.

What is joy?

The writer of the epistle to Galatians talked of the fruit of the Spirit as love, joy, peace, patience, kindness, goodness, faithfulness, gentleness and self-control.

Mother Teresa talked of a joyful heart as the normal result of a heart burning with love. Paul Tillich described joy as the emotional expression of a courageous 'Yes' to one's being. Joy is about accepting who you are, using your qualities to best effect while recognising that you are not perfect. It is acknowledging your imperfections and vulnerabilities and still being joyful within your own humanity.

There are times when you are more confident than ever before; when you make contributions that are more energised and go straight to the core of an issue; when you feel inspired by the actions of those around you and there is a step change in how you are able to contribute. All of these things can fill you with joy.

An inner sense of joy can create an upward spiral. When you feel at peace and joyful in yourself, you have the inner confidence to make a good contribution in a meeting or in the lecture room. Once you feel that your contribution is appreciated, the spiral goes on upwards and the sense of joy becomes stronger.

- How do you define joy?
- When do you feel most joyful?
- What increases that inner sense of joy?
- How can you create a strong continuing sense of inner joy that will help protect you at times when your energy is sapped and you feel that you are losing the goodwill of others?

Where does the sense of fun fit in?

Amanda held a sequence of leadership roles in the private and public sectors and had enjoyed some jobs more than others. The sense of fun in a job is important for Amanda in providing her with the lightness of touch that is one of her particular gifts. She described what gives her fun in a job as:

Talking to people and making connections between them. Joining things together, explaining things and engaging in dialogue. Building on understanding what makes people tick, and then seeing people grow and develop. Variety and dealing with new problems; feeling I can make a difference.

There are few things worse than a superficial joke or a teasing comment that completely misses the mark. Using humour effectively demands careful skill. It can be worth reflecting on the starting point that makes you and your colleagues smile. Is it:

- A sense of the absurd?
- The pleasure of shared endeavour?
- The glint in someone's eyes?
- The sense of what might have happened if a wall had fallen in?

Humour can be a valuable facilitator, particularly when you are nervous. I encouraged someone who was very nervous to imagine the people she was about to meet wearing pantomime outfits. If you can picture the rather severe chair of an interview panel dressed up as Little Bo

Peep, you can hardly fail to cope with the most serious of questions! This approach may sound trivial, but the more you can smile at yourself, the greater the likelihood that you will smile at others and the more they will be relaxed in your company.

Can you create a sense of joy in your team?

In the best teams there is a buzz with banter and laughter. How can you create that buzz in your team so that people are willing to go the extra mile when it is needed? Creating the right atmosphere is not straightforward, as humour can fall flat if used insensitively. Humour that flows well is built on good-quality personal relationships and a willingness to be teased.

Perhaps the simplest way of raising the spirits of colleagues is by simply smiling. Be conscious that everything about you gives a message to your organisation: not only your words, but your posture, facial expression, tone of voice and appearance. People will look for any signals that you feel things are out of control. When a CEO asked his chairman the single most important thing he should be doing, the reply was, 'Smile.'

Sometimes a leader's role is to be the 'cheerleader' for the team, particularly in turbulent times. This can be difficult and mean that you have to wear a mask, particularly if your role is a highly visible one. But continuing to appear confident and in control can be just the reassurance and uplift that your team needs. If you are able to look cheerful, most people you talk to will mirror your demeanour and end up smiling too!

Moving forward

➤ See joy as a special gift that you want to share with others.
➤ Recognise what makes you feel uplifted and enjoy the tonic.
➤ Allow yourself to smile and let it be infectious.
➤ See creating a sense of joy in your team as well worthwhile.
➤ Reflect at the end of each day on what has made you joyful.

Conclusion: Next Steps

In a fast-changing world it is essential to raise your game. It is not an option just to 'stand and stare'. So what are you going to do?

Key questions

The main thrust of this book has been the importance of a blend between self-belief and practical action. Self-belief comes from a combination of inner confidence and clarity about values; practical action is realistic, determined and planned. How do you want to respond?

Key questions to reflect on might be:

- What themes in the book have resonated most with me?
- Who am I going to talk them through with?
- What dated perceptions about myself am I going to leave behind?

- How am I now going to think differently about either the situation I am in or my capability to make a difference?
- What am I now going to do differently in practical ways?
- How is my definition of success changing?
- How am I going to live my values even more effectively?

Raising your game may be hard work, but it can be fun too! I encourage you to step up into whatever challenges you are facing with energy and confidence, building on your strengths, being grounded in your values and knowing what matters to you the most. Look for joy where you can and celebrate the companionship and support of those around you.

You can have much more of an impact than you might realise as you raise your game. Believe that you can have a significant impact for good as you look after your physical, emotional, intellectual and spiritual well-being. Be encouraged by your family, friends and supporters and give them the thanks that they deserve.

I hope that in some small way reading this book has changed you. Are you going to remember one idea, story or question from the book that will stay with you as you raise your game and step up? Maybe there is a choice you are now going to make that will set you on a different course or change your attitude. And remember to allow yourself moments of joy, whatever happens!

Selected Bibliography

Adair, J. (2005), *How to Grow Leaders*, London: Kogan Page.

Allan D., Kingdom, M., Murin, K. and Rudkin, D. (1999), *¿What if!: How to Start a Creative Revolution at Work*, Chichester: Captstone.

Archer, David and Cameron, Alex (2009), *Collaborative Leadership: how to succeed in an interconnected world*, Oxford: Elsevier.

Bibb, Sally and Kourdi, Jeremy (2004), *Trust Matters: for organisational and personal success*, Basingstoke: Palgrave MacMillan.

Boyatzis, Richard and McKee, Annie (2005), *Resonant Leadership*, Harvard: Harvard Business School.

Buckingham, Marcus and Clifton, Donald (2004), *Now, Discover Your Strengths*, London: Pocket Books.

Caplin, John (2008), *I Hate Presentations: transform the way you present with a fresh and powerful approach*, Chichester: Capstone.

Coffee, E. (2003), *10 Things that Keep CEOs Awake*, London: McGraw-Hill.

Collins, J. (2001), *Good to Great*, New York: Harper.

Covey, S.R. (1989), *The Seven Habits of Highly Effective People*, London: Simon.

Dawson, Heather (2007), *Thriving in a Faster Faster World*, London: Praesta.

Hammond, John S., Keeney, Ralph L., and Raiffa, Howard (1999), '*The Hidden Traps in Decision Making*', Harvard Business Review, September-October edition.

Hammond, John S., Keeney, Ralph L., and Raiffa, Howard (1999), *Smart Choices, a practical guide to making better life decisions*, New York: Broadway Books.

Handy, C. (1997), *The Hungry Spirit*, London: Arrow.

Ind, Nicholas and Watt, Cameron (2004), *Inspiration: capturing the creative potential for your organisation*, Basingstoke: Palgrave MacMillan.

Leighton, Allan (2007), *On Leadership*, London: RH Business Books

Lencioni, Patrick (2002), *The Five Dysfunctions of a Team*, San Francisco: Jossey-Bass.

Radcliffe, Steve (2008), *Future, Engage, Deliver: the essential guide to your leadership*, Leicester: Matador.

Seligman, M.E.P. (2002), *Authentic Happiness: using the new positive psychology to realise your potential for lasting fulfilment*, New York: Free Press.

Shaw, Peter (2005), *Conversation Matters: how to engage effectively with one another*, London: Continuum.

Shaw, Peter (2006), *Finding your Future: the second time around*, London: Darton, Longman and Todd.

Shaw, Peter (2008), *Making Difficult Decisions: how to be decisive and get the business done*, Chichester: Capstone.

Shaw, Peter and Linnecar, Robin (2007), *Business Coaching: achieving practical results through effective engagement*, Chichester: Capstone.

Shaw, Peter and Stephens, Jane (2008), *Riding The Rapids: how to navigate through turbulent times*, London: Praesta Partners.

Shaw, Peter (2006), *The Four Vs of Leadership: vision, values, value-added, vitality*, Chichester: Capstone.

Skelton, Arnie (2008), *Eliminating Stress*, London: Public Service Magazine, February–March edition.

Stone, Beverley. (2004), *The Inner Warrior: developing courage for personal and organisational change*, Basingstoke: Palgrave MacMillan.

About the Author

Peter Shaw is a Founding Partner at Praesta Partners, global leaders in executive coaching with offices around Europe, and in South Africa, Singapore and Australia. Their clients include senior people in the public, private and voluntary sectors, including senior civil servants, senior members of the Judiciary, ambassadors, Bishops and chief executives. Peter was formerly a director general within government and a member of five different government department boards. He also mentors staff in the colleges where he is a governor and people in his local community. He has written many articles on leadership and published a number of influential business books. Peter regularly leads workshops on the themes of his books in the public, private and voluntary sectors. He is a visiting Professor of Leadership Development at Newcastle University Business School.

Other books by Peter Shaw

Mirroring Jesus as Leader, Cambridge, Grove 2004

Conversation Matters: how to engage effectively with one another, London, Continuum, 2005

The Four Vs of Leadership: vision,values, value-added, vitality, Chichester, Capstone, 2006

Finding Your Future: the second time around, London, Darton, Longman and Todd, 2006

Business Coaching: achieving practical results through effective engagement, Chichester, Capstone, 2007 (Co-authored with Robin Linnecar)

Making Difficult Decisions: how to be decisive and get the business done, Chichester, Capstone, 2008

Riding the Rapids: how to navigate through turbulent times, London, Praesta, 2008 (co-authored with Jane Stephens)

Deciding Well: a Christian perspective on making decisions as a leader, Vancouver, Regent College Publishing, 2009

Forthcoming books

Effective Christian Leaders in the Global Workplace, Authentic, 2010

Defining Moments, Basingstoke, Palgrave/Macmillan, 2010

Index